Care and Conflict

Care and Conflict

Leaves from a Pastoral Notebook

KENNETH LEECH

Darton, Longman and Todd
London

First published in 1990 by
Darton, Longman and Todd Ltd
89 Lillie Road, London SW6 1UD

British Library Cataloguing in Publication Data

Leech, Kenneth *1939–*
    Care and conflict : leaves from a pastoral notebook.
    1. Church of England. Ministry
    I. Title
    262.143

    ISBN 0–232–51898–X

Phototypeset by Input Typesetting Ltd, London SW19 8DR
Printed and bound in Great Britain by
Courier International Ltd, Tiptree, Essex

Contents

Preface

This book contains the series of Pastoral Theology Lectures which I delivered in Durham University in February 1988. The first four chapters are virtually identical with the lectures as given, though I have filled out several areas which there was not time to develop. Chapter 5 draws together some material from the discussions I had with the students there and with others subsequently.

Many of the ideas in this book have appeared in a different form in articles in *The Independent, Third World Book Review*, in publications of the Jubilee Group, and in talks to various groups throughout Britain and the USA. Much of the material on drugs, on spirituality and on racism is developed in much greater detail in my other books and articles.

I am grateful to Professor Daniel Hardy for inviting me to give the lectures and for his hospitality and support during my time in Durham.

KENNETH LEECH

1

On the Edge

Ministry and Marginality

My aim in these chapters is to reflect on some aspects of my own pastoral ministry over the last twenty-five years, and to raise and discuss some theological and spiritual issues which arise from this experience. What I am offering – all I can offer – is personal, experiential theology: theology which has been tested and tried, much of it weighed in the balances and found wanting; much of it only held on to with great difficulty; some of it rediscovered in situations of great pain or of joy. It is therefore in one sense unbalanced as all contextual reflection must be. The contextual character of theological reflection, and the interconnection – and often conflict – between the personal and the 'received tradition' has been strongly emphasised in recent feminist theology. My experience has been that as one relates that which seems most deeply personal and uniquely so, one often finds that it makes connections, rings bells or arouses responses in others whose experience has been quite different.

Born and brought up in a poor working-class neighbourhood in the 'cotton towns' of Greater Manchester, I had no connection with the church until my teens. My move to London in 1958 to read modern history at King's College led to a deep and continuing relationship with the East End. It was in those undergraduate years that I became familiar with Cable Street, at that time the social centre of the London Docks, and this area was to become my home for some years. Indeed I have spent the last thirty years or so moving in and out of the same square mile of London's East End.

The growth of 'outcast London'

In 1883 *The Bitter Cry of Outcast London* was published. It was one of the most significant social documents of the nineteenth century and led to a massive growth of pastoral ministry and social reform in the East End and elsewhere. The concept of 'outcast London' referred to the existence within the city of zones of rejection, characterised by desperate poverty and decay. These areas were described and documented in an immense number of nineteenth-century documents – Mayhew's *London Labour and the London Poor*, Hollingshead's *Ragged London in 1861*, as well as Booth's massive *Life and Labour of the People in London*, published as the twentieth century dawned.[1] Here were the 'thieves' kitchens' described by Dickens, the slum alleys of the East End of which commentators wrote in fearfully dramatic terms; the 'darkest England' of William Booth. Here were districts such as Notting Dale which Dickens called 'a plague spot scarcely equalled for insalubriety by any other in London'. Here, he claimed, 'discontent, dirt, filth and misery are unsurpassed by anything known even in Ireland'.[2] Outcast London was never a racial ghetto though it included clusters of poor Irish and later the Jewish area of Whitechapel. Rather it encompassed districts in which were concentrated the long-term unemployed, the homeless, vagrant alcoholics, the ex-inmates of workhouses, prisons and asylums, alongside recent immigrants, migrants from depressed urban and rural areas, and a whole range of groups who were lumped together as 'the poor'. The poor were seen as another race, as less than human, a diseased and contaminating group. Booth termed them 'the residuum'.

For Marx they were the *lumpen*. The Communist Manifesto dismissed such communities of the very poor as 'that passively rotting mass thrown off by the lowest layers of old society'. They were unstable, parasitic, 'a whole indefinite disintegrated mass'. Engels called them 'the scum of the depraved elements of all classes which establishes its headquarters in the big cities ... the worst of all possible allies'. Anyone who worked with them was a scoundrel and a traitor to the movement.[3]

The geographical expression of social rejection was not peculiar to London: similar patterns were repeated in city after city: pockets of rejection, sometimes (but not always) correlated with a geographical neighbourhood – red light districts, twilight zones, 'bad areas'. In the post-war period Tiger Bay in Cardiff, Moss Side in Manchester and Liverpool 8 showed similar features to the marginal areas of London. These were the areas which, in the early years of Commonwealth immigration, became reception areas. What did not develop, in London or anywhere else, was a racial ghetto on the Harlem pattern. At the 1961 and 1971 censuses, while there were clusters of ethnic minorities in London, Birmingham, and other cities and towns, nowhere were there examples of even small areas resembling the American ghettoes. In Greater London in 1971, only five areas contained populations of which over one-third were of New Commonwealth origin.[4]

Since the Second World War the geographical expression of social rejection has intensified. New areas have been added to the old ones (such as Whitechapel or Notting Dale). Poverty and affluence have become increasingly contrasted. Since the late 1970s, divisions between rich and poor, affluent and deprived areas, have become much more sharp. The 'north-south divide' has become more marked, in spite of attempts to deny its existence or to oversimplify its character.[5] *Faith in the City*, the report of the Archbishop's Commission on Urban Priority Areas, used the concept of 'polarisation'. David Sheppard, Bishop of Liverpool, has spoken of 'the other Britain'.[6]

However, during the 1950s we were being told by many pundits that poverty was disappearing, as indeed was class. The 'withering away of class', the 'affluent worker', social mobility, were widely accepted themes. The city, in part, was seen as a site of regeneration and of hope. Urban conflict, it was claimed, was giving way to urban renewal. That optimism was to be short lived.[7]

In the early 1960s the urban sociologist Ruth Glass introduced two concepts into mainstream sociological discourse: gentrification and marginality. By gentrification she referred to the process by which areas which had been socially mixed were being occupied exclusively by the very rich, creating new upper-class ghettoes and ghettoes of the intelligentsia. The process began in Chelsea and Hampstead, then moved to Islington and parts of south London. In recent years it has spread to Spitalfields and other parts of the East End. The converse of gentrification was the uprooting of the poor, and the sharpening of the lines of demarcation between posh and poor neighbourhoods. Glass warned of the inevitable increase in 'marginal people'. What was likely to emerge was not a racial ghetto on American lines but rather 'ghettoes of "displaced persons" – of all kinds and shades'.[8]

The term 'marginal' had originally been used by the Chicago sociologist Robert Park in 1928 about the position of ghetto Jews in the USA. Glass used it in 1960 about communities which were cut off from resources and from power, locked into conditions of social inferiority and insecurity.[9] In their predicament lay the roots of future urban conflicts.

One of the earliest and most notorious such communities was in Cable Street, Stepney.

'Cablestrasse'

I went to live in Cable Street in 1958. The experience of living there for three years was to shape my future ministry to a powerful extent. By the 1940s Cable Street had become known throughout London as a 'coloured quarter' or 'London's Harlem', the heart of a badly-housed and neglected community of African and West Indian seamen, and the social centre of the London Docks.[10] It was the classic early marginal black colony. Ashley Smith called it 'the filthiest, dirtiest, most repellently odoured street in Christendom'.[11] But critics of the street often failed to recognise that there

4

was a community there. Among the seamen it was known as 'Cablestrasse'.[12]

Many writers commented on the atmosphere of the Cable Street café quarter. Writing in 1955, Michael Banton said that 'to the passer-by the area is a strange and definitely a frightening one; if he enters a café or a public house the other customers will scrutinise him thoroughly and there is an atmosphere so hostile that anyone but a coloured man, a seaman or one of the poorest of the local population will come to feel that he does not "belong" there and that he is not wanted'.[13] A more hostile and less accurate picture had been painted by Roi Ottley, a black American journalist, in 1952. Ottley wrote:

> Today, down by London Dock in about a square mile of back streets there exists a dismal Negro slum. The neighbourhood, situated in the Borough of Stepney, abounds with brothels and dope pads in old tumbledown buildings. Few slums in the US compare with this area's desperate character, unique racial composition, and atmosphere of crime, filth and decay.

Ottley went on to compare the Cable Street cafés with 'the good natured exuberance of a Negro tavern in Harlem'. By contrast in Cable Street 'the atmosphere resembled the Casbah in Algiers – mysterious, sinister and heavily-laden with surreptitious violence'.[14]

The hostility of Ottley's account was repeated in numerous sensational articles in the press from 1947 onwards. Thus Vivien Batchelor wrote in *John Bull* in 1947:

> Seamen all over the world know of Cable Street and if their tastes lie that way make for it as soon as their ships dock. Some of them are coloured boys just off their first ship. A few months ago they were still half-naked in the bush.[15]

In the same year the *Daily Mail* had written about the girls in the café quarter:

> The girls who haunt the cafés and pubs are not London

girls, they come from South Shields, Newcastle, Cardiff, Liverpool: many of them are on the run and some have escaped from remand homes. They are safe in Cable Street. Most of them are teenagers, they get drunk, and the coloured seamen they are with get jealous.[16]

The underworld of cafés and clubs in Cable Street reached its peak in the years 1958–61. Registered drinking clubs alone increased in Stepney from nineteen in 1954 to ninety-two in 1960, most of them in the Cable Street area. Clubs were often closed by the police and promptly reopened. One club was struck off the register in 1958. The following day a notice on the wall announced: 'The above club is moved from the register of clubs and has ceased to exist. Only members who have proved an asset will be invited to form a new club. Information and advice about a new club will be given to callers here most mornings between 10 and 11'. Not far away, The 9A Club was closed by the police. It became The Horseshoe and was soon closed again. Then it became The Corridor, and, when this was closed for a year, it became The Ninepins and stayed open. As The Corridor, the club boasted 666 members!

I lived in Cable Street for much of the period from 1958 to 1961. It was my introduction to London as an undergraduate, and I spent a good deal of time around the café society. During those years three East End priests were crucial influences on my ministry. The first was Father Neville, a shy, contemplative Franciscan pastor. Neville lived from 1944 to 1963 in an ex-brothel which had been transformed into St Francis Hospice. Like St Francis he believed that brothers 'should feel satisfied to be among the common and rejected people, the poor and the weak, the sick, the lepers and beggars of the street'.[17] Neville was committed to a life of contemplative prayer in the midst of this district of conflict and violence. He saw the work of prayer as central to the struggle with injustice and oppression, and his life and ministry was marked by prayerfulness and by a commitment to the broken and the oppressed.[18]

The second priest was Father Joe Williamson, the eccentric, extrovert, exhibitionist priest of St Paul's, Dock Street, who campaigned for slum clearance and for the care of women caught in prostitution. Father Joe was rarely out of the news, and had a tremendous flair for publicity. He was a crusader, and, like most crusaders, was infuriating to his colleagues and friends: unpredictable, impatient, often wildly inaccurate in his claims. Yet the extreme conditions in Cable Street called for such a person at that time. As a small child in Poplar, Williamson had come under the influence of the legendary Father Dolling, and in some ways he could be said to represent the end of the Dolling era. Yet while almost all of the slum ritualist priests were upper class and had public school and Oxbridge backgrounds, Williamson represented the tradition in reverse: the poor East End boy who had made it. His 'style', however, was that of the old paternalistic parish priest, always in cassock and biretta. He was a rugged individualist, 'non-political' in the party sense, and he held a strongly social view of the sacraments. Yet from another perspective Williamson was not a ritualist at all. He had nothing in common with the Anglo-Catholic party with its concern about valid orders, Anglican-Methodist unity, and (later) the ordination of women. His focus was the world, and while he himself was nourished by prayer and sacrament, he had no patience with, and probably no understanding of or interest in, the debates which concerned the Anglo-Catholic clergy who were his neighbours.[19]

The third priest was Stanley Evans, parish priest of Holy Trinity, Dalston. The most theologically and politically aware of the three, Evans was dominated by the theme of the Kingdom of God as a community marked by equality and justice, and of the eucharist as the expression of that community in terms of the local situation. Prayer and politics for him were held together in the eucharistic action. He was one of the pioneers of the parish eucharist at which all present received communion, and at Dalston the eucharist was always followed by a parish breakfast and discussion of issues arising from the sermon. Such an approach was virtually unknown in the 1950s outside one or two 'progressive' parishes.

Of the three, I think Evans was closest to myself in personality and temperament, and I saw in him my own weaknesses and strengths. He was extremely shy, and covered this up by an aggressive manner which often bordered on the insensitive and cruel. Yet in his personal ministry he was one of the gentlest men I ever knew. In public he was a ruthless debater and a fierce controversialist. I learned from him three lessons which have stayed with me through my ministry. The first was his insistence on the holiness of the common life. He totally opposed what he called 'the church condescending', and he really did believe in equality and in the dignity and value of working people. His whole spirituality and theology was rooted in the common life and the local community, and he had no time for elitism, preciousness and individualism. Secondly, he was an intellectual, and he put his intellect at the service of the movement. He was a living example of Gramsci's 'organic intellectual' who was a resource to, but also learned from, popular struggles and movements. He sought to overcome the gulf between intellectuals and ordinary life. Thirdly, he had a strong commitment to the English pub as a place of comradeship and pleasure, a place where the common life can be enjoyed and men and women can relax together.[20]

What I saw in these three men, in varying degrees, was a combination of contemplative prayer, pastoral compassion, political analysis and prophetic zeal. Those features have stayed with me and grown in importance over the years: they are vital to any balanced Christian ministry.

84 Cable Street, where I lived for a large part of my three years as a student, was a microcosm of a whole trend in pastoral care. As a Franciscan house of hospitality it was modelled very much on the approach developed in the USA by Dorothy Day and the Catholic Worker movement.[21] Later in the 1960s it became the first shelter for vagrant alcoholics and crude-spirit drinkers, set up by the newly formed Simon Community, a group which was also inspired by Dorothy

Day. Simon worked at rock bottom, at what was often termed a 'failure level'. It offered warmth, food, clothing and the love of Christ. But behind the ministry of 84 Cable Street, whether in its Franciscan period or in its Simon period after 1963, there were two important theological principles. The first was that prayer and action must be held together. The second was that any effective pastoral ministry must begin with *diakonia*, servanthood of a very humble and lowly kind. The symbol of such ministry was, and is, Christ's dirty towel. The church was before all else a servant church.

It was the experience of the Franciscan house in Cable Street which led me to write one of my first articles on ministry in the urban context. Entitled 'The church and the social outcast', it appeared in *Prism* in January 1964. In this article I tried to articulate some of the ideas which were to dominate my future ministry. London, I suggested, had become a society of conformists on the one hand, and of minorities of 'misfits' on the other. I argued that there was an urgent need for new forms of ministry among social outcasts in Britain's cities. I would stand by most of that article today, but there has been little progress since I wrote it.[22]

My early ministry

My ministry began in East London. After those early student years in Cable Street, I was ordained and became a curate at Hoxton where Dickens had written *Oliver Twist*.[23] I was there throughout the 'Mods and Rockers' period of the 1960s, the years of Carnaby Street and pep pills, of Harold Wilson and the Smethwick bye-election, and, in the Church of England, the years of John Robinson's *Honest to God*, of the Second Vatican Council and of 'South Bank religion'. These years were dominated musically by the Beatles, the Rolling Stones, The Who and The Kinks. It was in Hoxton that I became very heavily involved with young delinquents and, because of a close involvement with one parish family, with the growing community of heroin addicts.

9

From Hoxton I moved to St Anne's, Soho, as the drug culture escalated in 1967, and a major part of my ministry there was concerned with heroin addiction; with the problems of kids in the all-night clubs which were the centres of the traffic in pills; with pastoral care within the homosexual community; and with response to the growth of homelessness among the young. After teaching in Canterbury for three years, combining this with some ministry in Canterbury Prison and Dover Borstal, I returned to the East End, to Bethnal Green. Many of the issues raised by the years in Soho and Bethnal Green are discussed in Chapters 2 and 4. In this chapter I shall focus on one aspect of the Soho period: the emergence of what is often referred to by the curious term 'street ministry'.

Street ministry

The nightlife of Soho, as of many inner-city districts, centres on the streets. That is where the joy and the pain, the violence and the sadness, the darkness and the turmoil, are to be found. As a team of Christian workers in Soho, we felt that all pastoral ministry, all spiritual friendship, all theological reflection, had to begin at the street level. It seemed obvious. yet it called for an ascetical discipline of slowing down, standing still, and loitering. To loiter is defined in the Oxford English Dictionary as 'to linger indolently on one's way; to hang idly about a place; to dawdle over a task. Probably introduced into English by vagrants from the Low Countries'.

My own loitering was focussed particularly on three districts.

1. The clubs and bars

Soho in the 1960s contained a wide range of clubs. There were the old jazz clubs like Ronnie Scott's in Frith Street and The Bag of Nails in Kingly Street; discotheques of the early 60s type such as The Discotheque in Wardour Street, owned by Raymond Nash, The Scene Club in Ham Yard, and The Roaring Twenties in Carnaby Street; the large rhythm and blues and folk clubs such as The Flamingo and The Marquee, both in Wardour Street; and later the small folk clubs such as Les Cousins at 49 Greek Street and Bungies in Lichfield Street. But the clubs which attracted the young drug takers were the small, usually basement, 'coffee clubs', products of the middle 60s period. A few years earlier there had been a number of coffee bars which stayed open late at night – The French and the As You Like It in Monmouth Street, the Two I's in Old Compton Street, for example – and it was out of this coffee bar culture, itself a product of the late 50s, that the folk clubs and the coffee clubs developed.

The contemporary folk clubs in Soho grew up in the mid-1960s, Les Cousins and Bungies being the main ones, though a number of the other clubs ran folk nights. The rise of Simon and Garfunkel gave an added impetus to the growing movement. Paul Simon's first visit to Soho was in 1965 when he sang at a folk night at The Flamingo in Wardour Street. The event was organised by a well-known Soho figure called 'Curly' King, and the Ian Campbell Folk Group were top of the bill, with Simon, virtually unknown, at the bottom. He sang the Benedictus, in Latin (on his LP Wednesday Morning 3 a.m.), and it brought the house down! Judith Piepe, an extraordinary, self-appointed church worker, who specialised in working within the folk scene, was very impressed with this young man, and introduced him to the BBC. As a result of this encounter she recorded a series of talks on the BBC's religious programme 'Five to Ten'. The talks, each one accompanied by a Paul Simon song, were broadccast in Holy Week 1965, and they formed the basis of The Paul Simon Song Book. Judith wrote the preface to the printed version.

Paul Simon was to become the most famous of the singers who formed the Soho folk music network. Others included Al Stewart, Sandy Denny, and Bert Jansch. Al Stewart, in his early period, sang a number of songs which were social documentaries of events in Soho or the East End. Two songs are of particular importance in connection with this book, though they are hardly ever heard. 'Pretty Golden Hair' describes the suicide of a young homosexual, and is one of the most sensitive and disturbing songs about the consequences of rejection of gay people. The other, 'Who Killed Tommy McGeechy?', describes the true story of the death of a well-known methylated spirit drinker in police custody in Stepney. The folk clubs at this period contained many singers who commented on such events and issues.

By 1967 a small district around Berwick Street, Wardour Mews and D'Arblay Street in the northern part of Soho, just south of Oxford Street, contained the heaviest concentration of all-night coffee clubs: The Limbo, The Huntsman, The Coffee Pot, The LeDuce, The Rector's, The Stud, The Granada, The Student Prince, The Take Five, Koko's – all within a few yards of each other. (Further south, but part of the same network, was The Blue Gardenia in St Anne's Court and The Alphabet Club in Gerrard Street.) From loitering in this district there developed a ministry which included everything from coping with overdoses and sexually transmitted diseases to preparation for baptism and very long-term spiritual support. But it all began with loitering – being around, staying around, becoming a trusted person.

One curious aspect which is worth mentioning, but should not be taken too seriously, is that of the clerical collar. It is an issue about which clergy still get quite worked up, as the correspondence columns of church newspapers show. Although it is often seen as a 'traditional' form of attire, it is, like many allegedly traditional things, extremely modern, owing its origin to the nineteenth-century Rosminian priest Luigi Gentili.[24] I spent some time in 1967 weighing up the pros and cons of wearing a clerical collar in the Soho clubs. Would it turn people off, embarrass them, create unnecessary barriers and so on? In the end, I decided to wear it, for two main reasons: it would increase the speed at which I would become known and therefore build contacts, and it was the best way not to be mistaken for a plain clothes policeman. I quickly discovered that, far from putting people off, it was a vital pastoral contact point. Young people, seeing me in a club at 4 a.m., would frequently ask me whether I was a 'real vicar', or would tell me dirty jokes, or try to shock me. Others would enter into discussion about my motives, my sexuality, my credentials. Was I wanting to rescue people? Was I a grass (police informer)? Was I trying to pick them up? Others, in states of real or imagined distress, would introduce themselves. Soon many people would do so, having been informed by friends to look out for someone in a clerical collar. Some comments are memorable. Early one morning, as I was leaving The Alphabet Club in Gerrard Street, a very stoned girl looked at me with horror, and then laughed. 'Blimey,' she exclaimed, 'For a minute, I thought you was a vicar!'

Having said that, however, I must add that I have serious doubts about the value of the clerical collar in general. Once one has become known, it becomes less and less necessary, and more and more a hindrance. Many clergy seem to become unhealthily dependent on it as a kind of protection, and, like the parsonic voice and its accompanying mannerisms, it can easily undermine ordinary human contact. I rarely use one today though I often carry one around in case it comes in handy. But I am sure that a genuinely incarnational theology is best manifested in hiddenness and in the common humanity which does not depend upon, and does not place too much stress on, uniforms of separateness or professionalism.

The years in which I was working around the Soho clubs were also the years when detached youth work was beginning in Britain, and there was a considerable overlap between my work and that of the detached youth workers. I had already, in 1964, done some work in the East End with Derek Cox, one of the earliest detached youth workers in the country,[25] and with the Hoxton Café Project. In Soho, the Soho Project had been started in 1966 by Barbara Ward, who had previously been involved with the Teen Canteen in South London and with the Hoxton Café. Barbara Ward's work initially was in a large discotheque called Tiles in Oxford Street, though she spent a good deal of time also in the smaller clubs and amusement arcades. For a time the Soho Project took over the basement of St Anne's and ran The Plastic

13

Heart Club on Saturday nights. There was also the Rink Project, based at the Salvation Army Centre ('The Rink') at 275 Oxford Street, whose workers, Alistair Cox, Rod Moore, Peter Riddle and Norman Groves, were closely associated with our work. Further west there was the Portobello Project with Paddy McCarthy and later Geof and Tricia Bevan, and the Blenheim Project, both in Notting Hill.

Detached youth work owed its origins to experience with street gangs in American cities, though the structured gang model was quickly seen as inapplicable within the British context.[26] The shift from the language of 'unclubbables' to 'unattached' was seen in the important contributions from Mary Morse in 1965 and from Goetschius and Tasch in 1967. These books played a key role in establishing detached youth work as a recognised and valued trend within the structures of the youth service.[27] The term 'unattached' was used to refer to those young people who did not belong to youth clubs and did not use the youth service facilities. It was widely assumed that they formed a minority, and many people associated detached youth work exclusively with 'deviant' subcultures in the inner cities. But the Milson-Fairbairn report *Youth and Community Work in the 70s* showed that less than 30 per cent of young people were attracted by youth service provision. The unattached were in fact the majority of young people.

The youth workers who operated in inner London at the end of the 60s saw their work as 'youth work without any premises' (Geof Bevan). The Soho Project workers described themselves in 1972 as 'outreach workers', while some workers in Manchester used the term 'unreached youth'.[28] During these early years there was a lack of critical reflection on the ideology and practice behind the detached youth work approach. It was heralded in some quarters as a panacea for all the ills of young people. Yet in some respects the detached worker 'works from an even more menacing base' than the institutions which young people at least understand even if they reject them.[29] These words apply equally to the 'detached priest': it is of the greatest importance that one recognises the ambiguities and threats in the situation, and this calls for a high degree of honesty, sensitivity and recognition of the dangers of manipulation and subtle forms of control.

I began my pastoral work in the clubs in The LeDuce Club at 22 D'Arblay Street. This was a gay club run by Geoffrey Worthington, an eccentric character with a background in clinical psychology, and a microscopic knowledge of the West End. The LeDuce attracted a very large number of young male homosexuals from all over the south-east. There was a good deal of drug taking, mainly of amphetamines. Alone among the Soho coffee clubs, The LeDuce had its own welfare committee, of which I was for a time chairman: it included a lawyer, a nurse specialising in venereology, and a probation officer. At one period we ran a midnight advice centre on sexually transmitted diseases which acted as a valuable link with the local 'special clinic', James Pringle House at the Middlesex Hospital. The fact that I was not myself homosexual, and yet was seen to be sympathetic and tolerant towards the gay community, seemed to be a crucial factor in my being accepted, though a gay priest would have been able to achieve more in some areas, and would presumably have functioned differently.

The LeDuce in the late 60s was an integral element in the complex male homosexual culture of the West End which antedated the Sexual Law Reform Act of 1967 and the coming of gay liberation. The Soho gay scene grew up during the years when male homosexuality was illegal. Soho was the oldest of the 'ghetto' districts of London, the others being Chelsea, Earls Court and Notting Hill Gate. The 1970s was to witness the growth of the other three districts and the decline of Soho as centres of gay life. Within Soho the male homosexual community met in pubs, drinking clubs and coffee clubs, while the 'rent' (male prostitute) society focussed on Piccadilly. The gay pubs were fairly unpleasant and several were quite dangerous and 'rent'-based, though there were a number of gay bars which were friendly and relaxed. The drinking clubs tended to cater for older homosexuals who were often connected to the worlds of the theatre, art, music

15

and politics. It was the coffee clubs which provided the link between the old and the new cultures. They were an important transitional movement in the growth of gay social life and self-consciousness. The clientele was overwhelmingly young and there was a sense of excitement, fun and self-discovery. The openness associated with 'coming out' was present in germ, though the use of the Soho gay language, 'polari', was symptomatic and expressive of the fact that secrecy was still central to the culture.

After several months based in The LeDuce, I had established a weekly practice of regular two- to three-hourly sessions in the club, usually between 11 p.m. and 2 a.m., and from this developed links with the other clubs in the area which had different, but overlapping, clienteles.

It is important to emphasise, and it cannot be emphasised too strongly, that there was nothing innovative, 'trendy' or unusual about the ministry in the all-night clubs. I was doing nothing different from what priests and pastors do everywhere: being around, seeking to communicate the love of God, caring for people in distress, seeking to be a sacramental presence. The fact that my ministry was widely seen as unusual was a sad indication of the fact that so often priests and pastors were in the wrong places, distant from the needs of suffering people.

At the present time there is much debate about the church's response to homosexual people. This is not the place to add to the current controversies, but there are several aspects of the Soho experience which are worth emphasising. The first is the appalling situation which prevailed before the Sexual Law Reform Act of 1967. Nobody who remembers those years of fear, blackmail, corruption and intense psychic disturbance would wish to return to them. Yet there are signs of a hardening of prejudice, in which the church has colluded, which could lead in that direction. It was Michael Ramsey, then Archbishop of Canterbury, who, in the face of tremendous hostility and in spite of his own evident perplexity and revulsion in the face of homosexuality, steered the Act through the House of Lords as a matter of fundamental justice.

The second aspect of the Soho experience is the way in which the climate of fear and secrecy which created the gay ghetto helped to preserve immaturity. One young woman, Iris, whom I knew well in The LeDuce and who was a well-known figure in the gay scene in Soho in the late 60s, wrote about it in these words:

> The people on the scene now [1968] are all very young or they're all old, there's no in-between. . . They're all either very very young and been going for about six months or a year and think they know it all, think they're beautiful, but after a year they suddenly go to pieces . . . after having various affairs, VD, etc. . . . find they're spotty and aged and can't cope. . . I don't think anybody grows up on the gay scene at all. . . Whether they're a boy or a girl. They never grow up.[30]

There is no doubt that the discrimination against homosexuals created the atmosphere in which immaturity could be preserved. Yet my experience is that Iris's view is too pessimistic. Many of the young gay people in Soho did grow up in spite of the pressures against them, and some of the gay clubs did provide a healing and supportive climate for them.

In many ways, however, the church is still caught in the position which prevailed in society as a whole before the reforming legislation and the emergence of the gay liberation movement. Hence the terrible atmosphere of dishonesty and doublespeak which makes serious discussion of this issue virtually impossible in many church circles. Hence too the practical consequences of this atmosphere, described so well by John Fortunato.

> Lonely, isolated gay priests in remote backwaters quietly drinking themselves to death. Gay ministers trying to pastor – by definition, an intimate undertaking – but having to leave an enormous piece of their personhood outside the pastoral relationship. Quietly seething congregations who must deal with an evasive gay father who is present but never really present. Gay priests or ministers who vote

17

at church conventions or synods or conferences for the oppression of gay people in order to protect their reputations. There are literally thousands of clergy in such situations in the church today leading schizophrenic anxious lives. If we could only lift up their wholeness, how much blessing the church would know once again.[31]

Rowan Williams makes a similar point when he says that 'it is becoming harder all the time for a gay person to be *honest* in the church. We have helped to build a climate in which concealment is rewarded – while at the same time conniving in the hysteria of the gutter press, and effectively giving into their hands as victims all those who do not manage successful concealment.'[32]

In spite of all this, the history of the gay scene is marked by the presence of a dedicated network of priests and pastors who, in the face of the most overwhelming and disgraceful attempts to damage and discredit them, have maintained a faithful commitment to the pastoral care of the gay community. Priests such as Malcolm Johnson, David Randall, Bill Kirkpatrick, and many others deserve the gratitude of all people of compassion.

2. *The young homeless and the creation of Centrepoint*

The second type of loitering developed from our concern at the growing numbers of homeless young people in central London. We loitered around Euston Station, and met many young people from Glasgow and the north-east of England who began to descend on London at the end of the 1960s. It was our friendships with these youngsters, and our concern at their plight, which led to the foundation of Centrepoint in December 1969. Today Centrepoint is the major agency for young people who are homeless on the streets of London.

There were then, and for the most part still are, five main types of residential provision for the homeless in British cities: lodging houses; night shelters; voluntary hostels; statutory centres; and prisons and hospitals. There are, in addition, a range of social centres, soup runs and outdoor facilities, as

18

well as what are sometimes referred to as 'accidental' types of provision – railway stations, parks, and so on. Many homeless people in London since the early years of the twentieth century have opted for 'sleeping out'. The London County Council censuses from 1904 to 1949 give some indication of the trends. We were finding by 1970 that the numbers of people sleeping out in central London were as high as those for the 1920s.

During the time that I was in Soho, the types of provision for the homeless declined sharply. The numbers of lodging houses and cheap hostels fell from 567 in 1965 to 293 in 1972. But undoubtedly the main factor in the situation was the decline in cheap rented accommodation in London, a decline emphasised by John Greve's report for the London County Council in 1962.[33]

Although vagrancy is generally associated with the elderly, one of the main features of the late 60s was the growth of the number of juvenile vagrants or 'young drifters' as they were called in youth work jargon. The term 'young drifters' was used of those groups of young people who had declined to take up a fixed abode and had chosen to lead a 'disorganised life' in the West End. The first serious documentation of juvenile vagrancy was a report from the Blenheim Project of April 1966. Noting the increase in the numbers of 'out of town drifters', the report concluded that the real size of the problem was unknown. The old beatnik community in Trafalgar Square had grown up in the late 1950s. In 1968 Sally Trench in her best seller *Bury Me In My Boots* divided the beats into three groups: the permanent beats who never moved far from Trafalgar Square; the homing beats who went off on the road but always returned; and the wandering beats who never stayed in the same place for very long.[34] Some observers of Soho in the late 60s saw the 'young drifters' as the successors to the beats. Among them was the Salvation Army, based at 275 Oxford Street, known in the late 60s as 'The Rink'. The origins of the Rink Club and Rink Project went back to April 1966 when Chris Reid offered his services to the Salvation Army to work with young people in the streets of Soho. It

19

was from Chris Reid's work that the all-night Rink Club developed. Soon the street work was taken over by Alistair Cox and Peter Riddle, and within a short time the Rink Project, the second detached youth work project in the West End, had appeared. Cox and Riddle later took over the management of St Martin's Crypt in Trafalgar Square as a base for young drifters to sleep during the day and a centre for advice and support. The West End youth work with drifters had begun. In a survey in 1970 it became clear that 55 per cent of the clientele of the Rink Project came from five cities – 25 per cent from London, 13 per cent from Glasgow, 10 per cent from Liverpool, 10 per cent from Manchester, and 7 per cent from Dublin.[35]

However, it was equally clear that a much larger number of young people was arriving daily in Soho who did not fit the stereotype of the young drifter, young people who were quite new to the life of the West End. It was as a result of our concern at the growing numbers of young homeless, particularly in the City of Westminster, that we founded Centrepoint. There were two groups involved in its creation: St Anne's Church and the Simon Community. Simon, originally known as the 'mission to the misfit', had been founded by an extraordinary former probation officer, Anton Wallich-Clifford, in 1963. Its early work was with vagrant alcoholics and crude-spirit drinkers in the East End. I had worked closely with Anton and his colleagues both in the East End and in Soho, and I recall quite vividly an evening in November 1969 when we were having a drink together in De Hems pub in Macclesfield Street, Soho. I mentioned to Anton that our basement in St Anne's House was unused – deliberately because we had been led to believe that the house was likely to be demolished. Demolition had become an increasingly remote possibility. But the basement was damp, it was full of cockroaches, mice, and other vermin, and the electric wiring was faulty. Yet, I felt, we needed to renovate it and use it in some way for the increasing numbers of young homeless. Anton agreed. I asked him how much money Simon had in the bank. The answer was predictable: a deficit of

£8,000. I had £30. So we decided to open the basement as a joint venture in December.

It is worth reminding readers at this point that Soho is part of the City of Westminster. We found it necessary often to remind ourselves, for the City was as remote then from the realities of homelessness, and from the life of Soho as a whole, as it is now. On 22 April 1968 I gave a talk to the Westminster Christian Council, an ecumenical group of Christians in the area, on accommodation needs for young people within the City (see Appendix 1). A Social Responsibility Working Party, set up by the Council in 1967, had reported, to no one's surprise, that the most pressing need in the City was for accommodation for the large and increasing number of homeless young people. But, as is usually the case with church bodies, no progress was made, no further action was taken: a paper had been read, and the churches moved on to other business.

However, if the churches were barely awake to the situation, the position within the bureaucratic structures of City Hall in Victoria Street was unbelievable. On 3 April 1968, the Medical Officer of Health for the City of Westminster, Dr Briscoe-Smith, called a conference of people who were concerned with the care of homeless drug addicts in the City. One reason for calling this conference was a concern that 'unless a unified policy is agreed by all the parties concerned, there may be some overlapping of effort *and perhaps overprovision of services*, and this, of course, should be avoided' (my italics).[36] The good doctor need not have worried. Underprovision remained the norm, nothing at all resulted from the conference, though many people stressed the extreme urgency of the situation. Nor was this conference unusual. There is often an inverse relationship between the number of conferences and the degree of action over the issue under discussion. The relationship between Westminster and Soho was bizarre: to call it incomprehension would be an understatement. The statutory bodies with responsibilities in this area were, in my experience, extremely unhelpful and culpably ignorant, preferring to leave the hard work to voluntary workers. If

21

anything the City of Westminster has become even more callous and irresponsible in recent years. Today it does not even advertise its Homeless Persons Unit. According to one worker, 'It's one way of keeping people away'.[37] At no point in the period leading up the creation of Centrepoint can I recall the slightest hint of cooperation or interest from the staff of the City of Westminster. At least the Diocese of London looked on us with kindly supportive incomprehension.

The founding of Centrepoint was a major landmark in the campaign for the young homeless in Britain. Within the first two months we took in 600 people; in the first four months 1003; in the first year around 5000. By 1971 6025 people were admitted, of whom 18 per cent were from Scotland and 7 per cent from Glasgow.[38] The Irish percentage had also increased by 80 per cent between 1970 and 1971. In 1972 the total number of admissions had grown to 6508.[39]

During the years since we started Centrepoint there has been a massive increase in homelessness, in London and elsewhere, both among families and among the single. By the late 1970s the use of bed and breakfast hotels had increased to a tremendous degree,[40] while private rented accommodation continued to decline, falling by 7 per cent between 1981 and 1988.[41] Between 1970 and 1985, there was a 700 per cent increase in the numbers of the official homeless;[42] the real figures were much larger as all workers in the field knew. In 1985 it was estimated that there were around 50,000 homeless young people sleeping out or living in temporary accommodation in London. The Social Security Act of 1986, which replaced Supplementary Benefit by Income Support, made the position of the young homeless much worse. In 1986 John Greve showed that one-tenth of the population of the London boroughs (about 600,000 people) were homeless or had no secure home.[43] The numbers of homeless people has more than doubled since 1979. In 1989 figures from the Children's Society suggested that nearly 98,000 young people run away from home or local authority care each year.[44] That would be bad enough. What is perhaps even worse is the determination of the present regime to punish the homeless, even when they obey government advice. So government minister Nicholas Ridley advised the homeless in London to move elsewhere[45] though many of them had come to London in search of work. They had followed government advice and 'got on their bikes'. But 55 per cent of local authorities treated such people as 'intentionally homeless'.[46] A 1989 report from Centrepoint showed that the number of young people sleeping rough on London's streets had risen by more than 50 per cent in the past two years because of government benefit changes.[47]

To look back at those early years when we saw the problem emerging, when we warned, shouted, at times screamed at the authorities, is a painful experience. Today, in the harsh and cruel climate of Thatcherism, the situation of the homeless is far, far worse than anyone could have predicted in the 60s, as in the degree of incomprehension (or wilful refusal to understand) in government. But Centrepoint goes on. In a cold and callous climate, it is just as well it is there. At least it offers a bed for the night. But, as Brecht wrote and as we always knew, this does not, by itself, end the age of exploitation.[48]

3. Piccadilly

The third area was Piccadilly itself. 'The Dilly' was a meeting place of subcultures. There was the heroin addict area around the Haymarket exit of the underground station next to the all-night Boots' chemist, known as 'junkies' corner'. Nearby was the all-night Friar Tuck coffee bar where young drifters and old down and outs would spend all night over one cup of coffee. There was Playland, the amusement arcade which was later to become notorious as a result of publicity on the Yorkshire TV programme 'Johnny Go Home' in May 1975. There was the stretch of railing by the corner of Regent Street, known as the 'meat rack' or the 'meat market', where the rent boys, homosexual prostitutes, would hang out.[49]

More than anywhere else the Dilly was the place of polarisation. West of Piccadilly Circus one entered the world of the

Carlton Club, The Athenaeum Club and The Constitutional Club; east of the Circus was the world of The Alphabet Club, The Limbo Club and The Flamingo Club. The world of the Royal Academy, Fortnum and Masons and Jermyn Street to the west, and that of the strip clubs, the junkies' corner and the prostitutes simply did not meet. The statue of Eros was a symbolic point. The boundary between the parishes of St Anne, Soho and St James, Piccadilly ran through the middle of it. We used to say that if you called it Eros it was in the parish of Soho; if you called it the Shaftesbury Memorial, it was in St James's parish. It was a most important cultural divide. On one occasion the Bishop of London, Gerald Ellison, visited the parish late at night with the church-warden, a well-known local probation officer. As they stood close to Boots', an addict greeted the probation officer, and, when he was introduced to 'Dr Ellison', responded: 'Pleased to meet you, Dr Ellison. I'm at Dr Saville's clinic myself. Which clinic are you from?'

The ministry of loitering and listening was both a purgative and illuminative time, a time in which one was constantly shaken, humbled, humiliated and amazed. Throughout our ministry with individuals we were aware of our own vulnerability, we were thrown back upon our own inner crises, and our own wounds often began to bleed. Our own brokenness became central to our ministry and to our theology: it was a painful and transforming experience.

Today I see close parallels in the experience of my colleagues who are now involved with sufferers from AIDS. This is particularly true in relationship to the experience of moving from a position where one is in control to one where one is very exposed and very vulnerable. So a priest who has recently spent a long period working on an AIDS ward in San Francisco writes:

After seventeen years as a London parish priest where my ministry has been built upon the ongoing building up of relationships and community development centred on the eucharistic community, I have found it especially hard adjusting to the ministry on the AIDS unit . . . where each encounter must stand on its own; where each opportunity is special; and where time is not on our side. Learning that 'to be' exposes me to my own frailty, loneliness and nakedness, especially perhaps as a stranger in a far country. I have always been a great fixer, both as social activist seeking to change the world; and as the priest-actor-manager offering a sacramental merry-go-round of exciting worship and meaningful spiritual comfort. Only now am I slowly, falteringly and gratefully facing the challenge of staying where the suffering really is; of not knowing the answers, and being honest about this; of allowing others to set the agenda for ministry; and even admitting that I receive from them as much as I can ever give.

This priest goes on:

Pastoral involvement means learning what it is to share the powerlessness, the fear and the degeneration which HIV brings to innocent sons and daughters made in the image of God. It is a road to Calvary, not knowing answers; moving slowly, falteringly and fearfully, staying with pain as it really is: with the rotting bodies, the decaying brains, the disabled forms; the prematurely aging human frames, the broken hearts of the medics and nurses as well as the dying and their loved ones; the terrified youth realising he's almost dead before beginning to live. There can be no neat answers, no religious platitudes. Yet in some mysterious way we are used as icons, sacraments, models of the God who hung on the cross.[50]

I have quoted this passage at length because it rings so many bells, and connects so closely with my own experience in Soho. It has been said that AIDS has 'opened a Pandora's box of unfinished spiritual business'.[51] But that box was opened in the 1960s and the issues which it brought to the surface have still not been adequately confronted. Two areas are of particular importance.

First, the sense that time is not on your side. That sense can become an occasion for proselytising of a cruel and exploitative kind. The dying are particularly vulnerable to such exploitation, a kind of spiritual rape. However, the sense that time is not on your side can become a way of learning the pastoral meaning of patience, of waiting and of silence. Linear time (*chronos*) can be crisis time (*kairos*). The *chronos* of dying can be a *kairos* of the spirit. The person in crisis can be helped and strengthened by the pastor who is able to practise the discipline of attention, of waiting, and who has learned something of the language of silence. Much of our ministry in Soho was silent.

One of the people from whom I learned much about the pastoral value of silence was a man called Harry Trinder. Trinder was an integral part of the Soho underworld, and was involved in managing a number of the clubs in the Berwick Street district. At any hour of the day or night, one was likely to find him leaning on a bollard at the corner of Berwick Street and D'Arblay Street: it became known as 'The Leaning Bollard of Trinder'. (It is still there!) Once when he was asked what he did, he replied, 'I'm a borough surveyor' and that was exactly what he was. He surveyed the borough, and nothing passed him by. Trinder was a godsend in pastoral work, for he knew what was going on, knew what had happened to people. He kept his ears to the ground, and he missed nothing.

Secondly, the sense that, confronted with the sufferer at the point of desperation or even death, one is on holy ground. That sufferer has perhaps seen things which you have not seen, learned lessons about love and suffering and sacrifice, about loneliness and rejection and pain, about solidarity and frailty and imperfection, and about hope and transformation – very quickly. It is the time to refrain from slick comments and to learn from the sufferers who have had thrust upon them 'the most profound kind of priesthood',[52] the confrontation of death.

To minister at this level is to allow oneself to become very vulnerable, very shaken. It is to learn the truth of Alastair Campbell's words:

> As we seek more deeply for those resources of help and guidance which we have to offer others in pastoral care, we find them in a surprising place – in our vulnerability. . . Such a relationship does not depend primarily upon the acquisition of knowledge or the development of skill. Rather it depends upon a caring attitude towards others which comes from our own experience of pain, fear and loss and our own release from their deadening grip.[53]

What I have described is one way in which we are challenged, wounded and healed by pastoral care in crisis, which becomes critical for us also. We do not emerge from this experience unaffected. Like Jacob, wrestling with the angel, we emerge limping. If henceforth we are to be healers, we are to be wounded healers.

Some harmful Christian responses

Much Christian ministry never seems to reach this point. It is held back by fear: fear of closeness and contamination; fear of sexuality, a fear which is very deeply rooted in the church; fear of taking risks; and fear of the possibility of loss of control. So ministry becomes genteel, careful and at one remove, geographically and emotionally, from the real needs of people. Because of fear, ministers avoid the places where people are, and where critical decisions are made, or they protect themselves from the possibility of hurt and change by the acquisition of false certainties.

One way of coping with fear of any real closeness to people is through the cultivation of the crusading mind. The crusading mind is sure of everything. It is utterly secure. It has God taped. Soho was littered with crusaders. They were drawn to it as wasps to a jampot. At times the Dilly seemed full of them. Most of the crusaders saw the neighbourhood and its inhabitants as an epicentre of concentrated sin and sought, by preaching, the distribution of tracts and other means, to draw individuals away from it. They were in a hurry. They never stayed to listen, to get to know the people, to learn of their feelings, hopes, fears, desires, joys. By their insensitivity and their loudness, their aggressive approach to people already badly damaged, they did incalculable harm to their victims, to themselves and to the credibility of the Christian church. They left the Christians on the spot to pick up the pieces. With the advent of AIDS and the resurgence of homophobia, they are back again, having apparently learned nothing over those long sad years. For with the advent of AIDS we have experienced 'the most sordid and squalid campaign of bigotry and scapegoating which this country has seen since the heyday of Mosleyite enthusiasm'.[54]

The crusading mind, says Kosuke Koyama, is entirely opposed to the crucified mind. The crusading mind is rooted in fear and the intolerance which is born of fear. Its aim is to destroy. The crucified mind is rooted in love and suffering: its aim is transformation through sharing the pain.[55]

The other way in which Christians avoid that vulnerable wounded closeness is by a kind of liberal professional kind of caring which is detached, skilful, and keeps its distance. While very different from the crusader with whom the liberal pastor feels no affinity, they have at least this in common: they are in control of their material. They have acquired the skills of pastoral care. They are efficient managers, distributors of resources. Carl Wennerstrom wrote of the liberal style of pastoral care:

Metaphorically speaking the first liberal (so far as the distance goes at any rate) might well have been the man who helped Jesus carry the Cross to the place where he was crucified. With a job to be done, he was there. With energy to be spent, he had it. And in carrying a heavy cross, he was not drawn too close together with Jesus. Once the spot had been reached and the outcome was certain he dropped from sight; we hear no more of this early liberal in the New Testament. Perhaps he was off to the Circuit Court, hoping against hope to get a reversal of the conviction and having the courage to try. Or he may have been investigating the future support of Jesus's family or the burial arrangements, or he may even have been getting up a petition to Rome about Pilate. What he was about was no doubt of great potential significance. But at the place of crucifixion he was absent once the cross had been delivered. For a liberal the optimal social distance.[56]

I believe that the liberal professional model of pastoral care has done incalculable damage to our whole understanding of the nature of care, and has damaged many individuals in the process. It has led to the emergence of a whole empire of paid carers, has institutionalised the concept of care within a bureaucratic 9 to 5 pattern, and has undermined that basic human love which is central to the Christian tradition. The promotion of bureaucratic and managerial approaches by bishops and clergy trainers in recent years must be viewed with the greatest suspicion and subjected to the most ruthless theological critique. In Soho, it would have been of no use whatsoever.

At the heart of both the crusading and the liberal professional approach is a desire for tidyness and a kind of purity, a revulsion against mess. So much religious life is influenced and dominated by a concern for purity. The fear of sexual contamination in particular goes very deep. The exclusive wing of Christianity has been obsessed with it since early Christians refused to accept those with uncircumcised penises. Today people with AIDS suffer a multiple stigma, for they carry in their bodies both the physical marks (blotches, weight loss, skin diseases) and the sense of emotional rejection. They are the contemporary equivalent of the lepers of New Testament times, and the concern to avoid contamination by lepers of all kinds runs through the Christian tradition. Yet if we look at the ministry of Jesus we find exactly the opposite: it is by closeness to and solidarity with the outcasts that he pursues his work of proclaiming the nearness of the Kingdom of God.

The ministry of Jesus

The ministry of Jesus, as described in the Synoptic Gospels, begins with the marginal people of Galilee and from there moves to Jerusalem, the seat of the mighty and powerful. He starts with the peasants, and only then, in their company, moves to the centre of power. The destitute, the unclean and ritually impure, the hopeless, the frustrated zealot militants, as well as the feverish, the blind, the paralysed and the lepers, are gathered together to form the core of the new messianic community. Jesus in fact creates a community of riffraff, and he who was himself born in the outhouse of an inn offers grace to those who had no hope of participation in the eschatological banquet.

It is these people, the excluded and the dispossessed, whom Jesus calls, and with whom he shares a common meal. This sharing of a meal was at the very heart of his ministry, his *diakonia*. So central is the meal in Jesus's ministerial style and method that it is astonishing how neglected it has been in pastoral reflection. There is no chapter of St Luke, for example, in which food is not mentioned, and the shared meal to which all were invited plays a central part not only in the actual ministry of Jesus but in his parables of the Kingdom. Thus in Luke 14:1–24 we have the parable of the great banquet. Here Jesus teaches his disciples:

> When you give a dinner or a banquet, do not invite your friends or your brothers or your kinsmen or rich neighbours, lest they also invite you in return, and you be repaid. But when you give a feast, invite the poor, the maimed, the lame, the blind, and you will be blessed, because they cannot repay you. You will be repaid at the resurrection of the just.

The significance of this invitation is easily missed by the modern reader. In the Levitical code, those forbidden access to the sacred food were the blind, the lame, those with mutilated faces, those with limbs too long, those with injured feet or hands, hunchbacks, dwarfs, those with sight defects, itch-

ing diseases, scabs, crushed testicles, or any blemish (Lev.
21:17–23). Similarly, in the rite of Qumran, those afflicted in
the flesh, the crushed, lame, blind, deaf and dumb, those
with defective eyesight, and the senile might not attend the
messianic banquet (1 Q. Sa. 2:5–22). It is this bias against
those with handicaps and disabilities which Jesus reverses,
and this becomes a cause of scandal. Indeed it is fair to say
that Jesus was killed because of the way he ate and the
company he kept. His enforced isolation on Calvary was the
climax and conclusion of a ministry of subversive closeness.[57]

The struggle on the cross was the outcome of a life of
struggle and conflict. The crucifixion outside the gate in the
company of criminals was the culmination of a life lived on
the edge, as a friend of the rejected, and, as the outcast leper
was forced to live outside the camp (Lev. 13:46), so Jesus
died outside the camp. And it is there that we must follow
him and serve him. 'Therefore let us go forth to him outside
the camp, and bear the abuse he endured' (Heb. 13:13). In
Christian discipleship there is a constant need to 'turn back
to the condemned and rejected'. Indeed conversion itself is a
case of 'always turning to the victim'.[58] It is there that God
is found.

The Christology of Diakonia

In all that I have written, there are two central Christological
truths. The first is the truth that Christ is found, now as then,
among the poor and lowly, on the edge, at the margins. The
second truth is that to be *en Christo*, to be icons of Christ, we
need to follow his way of lowly servanthood, and because
Christ is found among the poor, our response to the poor
becomes both a diagnostic test of our Christological orthodoxy, and a sign of judgment. As the Bishop of Durham has
written:

The way the poor are treated as less than human reveals
the essentially dehumanising trends at work throughout

31

society. Thus the poor (in the extended sense to take in the marginals and the excluded and not just the physically grossly underprivileged) are not just *a* problem of society. There is focussed in them, in their flesh and blood and their deprivations, *the* problem of society. It is in this sense that they are signs of the judgment of the Kingdom.[59]

What I have been putting forward is, in Latin American theology, endorsed by Pope John Paul II and the Roman Catholic Bishops, termed the 'preferential option for the poor'. The American Roman Catholic Bishops, in their Pastoral Letter on the economy of the USA refer to it as 'the social and ecclesiological counterpart of the emptying (*kenosis*) of Jesus in the incarnation'.[60] The option for the poor has nothing to do with any supposed innate moral goodness of poor people, or any innate sinfulness of rich people. Nor has it to do with a paternalistic and condescending idealising of poverty. It has to do with recognising that the Kingdom of God of the gospels only comes by a reversal of relationships, and therefore of structures, a putting down of the mighty and an exaltation of the lowly. In this sense God is one-sidedly the God of the poor and lowly.[61] It has to do with recognising that the real values and priorities of any society are exposed and manifested in its victims. As R. H. Tawney pointed out, there is no criterion which reveals the character of any social philosophy more clearly than the way in which it treats those who fall by the wayside.[62]

Christ is found among the poor and lowly. He is squeezed out of the mainstream onto the edge of society, and can only be found there alongside its other victims. It was a truth which Thomas Merton saw in his solitude and his solidarity with the marginalised people of the world.

Into this world, this demented inn, in which there is absolutely no room for him at all, Christ has come uninvited. But because he cannot be at home in it, because he is out of place in it, and yet he must be in it, his place is with those others for whom there is no room. His place is with those who do not belong, who are rejected by power because they are regarded as weak, those who are discredited, who are denied the status of persons, tortured, excommunicated. With those for whom there is no room, Christ is present in this world.[63]

Merton believed that the marginal position of his own monastic vocation enabled him to experience a solidarity with, and understanding of, other marginal people and groups. I will have more to say about Merton's contribution to our contemporary pastoral understanding in Chapter 3. For me, his concept of the monk as a marginal person, one who 'withdraws deliberately to the margins of society with a view to deepening fundamental human experience',[64] was applicable to much Christian ministry beyond the monastic community. Ministry to those whom society has rejected and marginalised must begin with a recognition and an exploration of our own marginal status as Christ's disciples.

Any authentic theology which is truly incarnational and passionate (passion-centred) must begin with a conscious act of solidarity with, learning from and standing by the people in one's neighbourhood who are at the bottom, the really helpless, the crushed and broken people. There is nothing romantic or dramatic about this. There is much pain, much personal upheaval, but a tremendous joy, liberation and release. More than that: there is a unique insight into the workings of the social order as seen from the underside of history. As Bonhoeffer wrote many years ago:

We have learnt to see the great events of world history from below, from the perspective of the outcast, the suspects ... the powerless, the oppressed, the reviled – in short, from the perspective of those who suffer.[65]

2

Opium of the People
Ministry and Drug Cultures

In Chapter 1 I reflected on the Christian ministry which is located 'on the edge', on the margins of 'respectable' society, and on the centrality of the rejected in the ministry of Jesus and of his followers. One of the most rejected communities with which I have been deeply involved over the years is that of heroin addicts, or, more accurately, of addicts to the needle. The folk singer Bert Jansch, whose songs were extremely popular in the Soho of the 1960s, wrote a song called 'Needle of Death'. The final words were:

> Through ages man's desire
> To free his mind, to release his very soul,
> Has proved to all who live
> That death itself is freedom for evermore,
> And your troubled young life will make you turn
> To a needle of death.

Bert Jansch's theme is that the attraction of heroin is related to a combination of the desire for release, for freedom, for liberation, on the one hand, and to a sense of frustration, confusion, and despair on the other. So the needle becomes a slow form of suicide. The frustration turns to violence and is directed internally, towards oneself. In this tension between release and despair, the needle acts as a kind of microcosm of much of contemporary western culture.

In this chapter I want to discuss some of the changes which have occurred in the drug scene in Britain over the past twenty-five years; and to reflect on the insights which have come to me through ministry among drug users into the nature of priesthood and of pastoral care.

Two drug cultures: Soho and Haight-Ashbury

In January 1970 I attended the international conference of Free Clinics in Haight-Ashbury, San Francisco. For some years a number of us in Soho had been making contact with people working in the San Francisco area, to see what we could learn from one another, and to share ideas and experiences, and a steady movement of workers had developed between the two cities.

These two districts, Soho in London and Haight-Ashbury in San Francisco, stand out as epicentres of drug abuse in their respective cities. Each has acquired a wider significance through international youth culture and their impact on thousands of young people is very considerable. Around both districts a whole mythology of false stereotypes has been built up.

The two districts are in fact very different in their social and cultural history, in their history of drug use, and in many other ways. But there are some important similarities and parallels which throw light on the shape of pastoral ministry among drug takers and on what was to become known as the 'counter-culture'.[1] Today it is fashionable to dismiss the 1960s as a cul-de-sac, a false path, a mistake.[2] I want to suggest that we cannot make sense of our predicaments today without recognising the immense upheaval and the immense creative forces of that decade, and seeking to learn from them, to build upon them, and to move beyond them.

Haight-Ashbury was the centre of the hippy movement. As one of their own poets wrote:

> O beautiful for hairy beard,
> For psychedelic smiles,
> For stroboscopes and costumes weird
> And runaway juveniles.

Haight-Ashbury, Haight-Ashbury,
America unbound!
Within thy good old neighbourhood
The rising underground.[3]

The influx into Haight-Ashbury increased in the summer of 1967. On the 13 June 1967 the San Francisco Deanery Clergy issued a statement.

The church must take the hippie movement seriously. . . These young people are saying something. . . If the church simply condemns the subculture for drug abuse or for vagrancy or for uncleanliness or for irresponsibility (whatever that may be) it falls into the position of defending intrinsic values – values which need no defending if they do indeed exist. If the church is really to exercise its prophetic ministry, it must be open to communicate the real message of the new Haight-Ashbury community to the world and to communicate the gospel of freedom, to the Haight-Ashbury.[4]

In Britain Major Fred Brown of the Salvation Army assured us that 'the true flower child' was 'a responsible member of society, holding down a steady nine to five job'.[5] Caroline Coon, the founder of Release, told us that the hippy was 'the product of a society whose moral spirit is lower and more disillusioned than it has been for some time'.[6] Even the occasional monk conceded that 'we have let ourselves be subverted by utopia and can never be the same again'.[7]

'Summer of Love'

The summer of 1967 was crucially important. In Britain Scott Mackenzie's record 'San Francisco' was at the top of the record charts. San Francisco was portrayed as a kind of paradisal state where beautiful people with flowers in their hair wandered dreamily in an Eden of flowers and LSD. 'Make love, not war' was the slogan of that summer. The origins of the 'summer of love' lay in the Haight-Ashbury psychedelic culture of the previous year. It was the arrival of Ken Kesey and his Merry Pranksters in San Francisco which made LSD known throughout the world, and transformed an elitist cult into a global counter-culture.

Kesey probably first took LSD in August 1965. From this date onwards he and his group moved around the cities of the West Coast and introduced people to 'the Acid Test'. Out of the combination of LSD and electronic equipment came the 'San Francisco Sound' which was soon to transform American pop music. Among the first converts to LSD were the Thelin brothers who opened the world's first psychedelic shop in Haight Street on 1 January 1966. Two weeks later Kesey hosted a Trips Festival with 15,000 people. Haight-Ashbury became the centre of a new youth world. Acid rock, with such groups as Jefferson Airplane and the Grateful Dead, was born.[8]

Meanwhile in Britain the Beatles produced 'Sergeant Pepper' on 1 June. The Beatles were of crucial importance to the counter-culture in both countries. The American poet Allen Ginsberg called Liverpool 'the center of the consciousness of the new universe'.[9] At the same time Simon and Garfunkel and Bob Dylan were moving from old style folk protest music towards the exploration of the inner world, while at a more intellectual level R. D. Laing's *The Politics of Experience and The Bird of Paradise* and the works of Herbert Marcuse were selling well.

I moved into Soho during the 'summer of love', living in a flat just behind Carnaby Street. The place rang with bells and beads, and was filled with young people in kaftans and amazingly beautiful clothes – 'gentle people with flowers in their hair'. Many people today write off that summer, and the era which it focussed, as idealist fantasy, utopian illusion. One writer has claimed that the radical wing of the Labour Party became 'hijacked by hippiedom' and lost contact with ordinary people.[10] My view is that much of the creative and hopeful side of our society today owes its origins to people who were inspired and shaped by that period. It was a period

37

of alternative vision, of hope, of creative disaffiliation, a time for seeing visions and dreaming dreams.

For me, however, there was also a destructive side to that summer. In May 1967 Lady Isabella Frankau died. Both her death and her name meant little to the country as a whole, but the effect on the drug scene was catastrophic. Lady Frankau had been the most eminent of the 'junkies' doctors' for some years. Some would claim that she controlled heroin addiction in the capital. She was the doctor who was cited in a government report, though without naming her, as having prescribed six kilogrammes of heroin in 1962. The immediate effect of her death was to release hundreds of addicts on to the illicit market. At this point there appeared a curious figure who was to play a strange role in my life for some years until his death in obscurity in February 1981: Dr John Petro.[11] When he died he had been utterly forgotten. But in 1967 and 1968 he was front page news in all British newspapers and one of the most hated men in Britain.

John Petro was the most notorious, and among the last, of the 'junkies' doctors', that small group of physicians who managed heroin and cocaine addiction in Britain until the Dangerous Drugs Act of 1967 took the prescribing of these drugs out of their hands. The Second Interdepartmental Report on Drug Addiction of November 1965, the Brain Report, argued that 'the major source of supply has been the activity of a very few doctors who have prescribed excessively for addicts', claiming that 'not more than six doctors' were involved.[12] I knew most of the junkies' doctors, and have written about them elsewhere.[13] What distinguished Petro from the others was not that he was uniquely irresponsible, or that he prescribed uniquely large amounts of drugs – and it certainly was not that he made large amounts of money from addicts. (By February 1969 he was living on £8 a week dole money.) It was that he prescribed the drugs from Baker Street Underground Station, from the pavement outside Boots' all-night chemist at Piccadilly Circus, and from the Friar Tuck Coffee Bar in Coventry Street. He was a barefoot doctor, who was as much a part of the criminal subculture as any addict. In 1968 he was struck off the medical register. His departure, with the related legislation and policy changes, brought an era of drug control to a end. Within a short time the criminal syndicates had taken over the heroin scene which escalated far beyond anything we had envisaged.

Petro's strange role in the history of British drug abuse, and my friendship with him, forced me to reflect on my own role as a priest seeking to care and minister within the same drug culture. What was I doing? Were the two of us all that different as we sought to comfort the afflicted, to bind up the wounded, to treat the immediate crisis, to preserve damaged and broken people for another day? Both of us were engaged in ambulance work, in sticking plaster ministry: both of us worked at a failure level. Were we wrong to do so?

As the years have gone by I have often pondered on the dilemma with which Petro faced me. In caring for the street addict, was I doing more than merely reinforcing a destructive life style? Often that is what I seemed to be doing. Yet I was able to operate within a framework where change was poss-ible, and where positive and supportive networks were seeking to reduce the destructive forces within the culture. In Soho, at the point of crisis, the ambulance role was of crucial import-ance. St Anne's, and the detached work in the streets which spread out from it, was in many respects the pastoral equival-ent of a hospital casualty department, and clearly by itself it would have been woefully inadequate.

The growth of the helping agencies

In Haight-Ashbury, the founding of the Free Clinic led to a whole movement of health care, while, across the bay in Berkeley the Free Church operated under its remarkable pastor Dick York, one of the pioneers of street ministry in the American counter-culture. The Free Church of Berkeley operated a crash pad service and a 24-hour switchboard, dealing with drug and related crises. In this provision it laid the foundation for the later developments of rape crisis centres, gay switchboards, and so on. In London, organisations such as Release and BIT grew out of the experience of 1967. Our own centre at St Anne's House, at 57 Dean Street in Soho, began to operate in 1967 as a centre within Soho where heroin addicts were accepted and helped; and as a centre from which a ministry developed among drug takers in almost all of the all-night clubs in the West End as well as around the 'junkies' corner' at Piccadilly.

One of our earliest concerns was with the provision of accurate and reliable information on drug abuse to counteract the hysterical and ill-informed material which was circulating widely. In 1967 Brenda Jordan and I produced a small book entitled *Drugs for Young People: their use and misuse* as a text book for use in schools' current affairs classes.[14] It was the first of its kind, and for many years it remained the only such text which was addressed to school pupils. We realised that no information is neutral or value-free. To provide information with no context is useless or dangerous. Yet my experience has been that far more young people are damaged as a result of ignorance, sometimes deliberately promoted by the mass media and the crusaders, than are damaged by accurate knowledge. In no area has the need for accurate information been so necessary as in that of drug use, yet no area has been so plagued by falsehoods and fictions.

Part of the task of information provision was the dissemination of details of sources of help. In 1965 I produced a duplicated sheet entitled *Drug takers: who can help?* It was a confidential document, and contained lists of people, mainly my friends and colleagues, with details of the kind of help they thought they could give. The demand for this was enormous. By 1967 it had grown to a printed document, published first with the help of the journal *Education*, and then by the Church of England Council for Social Aid as an appendix to a booklet on drug dependence. By the 1970s it had become a book entitled *Drug Aid* and this led eventually to a major directory published by the Standing Conference on Drug Abuse.

Linked with this directory and other printed sources was

our Tuesday night open seminars at St Anne's House. A prison medical officer, himself a regular attender, wrote of these seminars that they attracted 'a quite extraordinary array of international experts on drug addiction. The audience was as likely to contain a government assistant secretary as a hippy, an eminent psychiatrist as an interested member of the Women's Institute from Hampshire'.[15] The seminars were a remarkable phenomenon. Beginning as a self-help strategy of the Soho Drugs Group, a loose network of workers formed in 1967, the original idea was that of educating one another on aspects of drug use and abuse. We gathered together a variety of workers in the Soho district, youth workers, social workers, probation officers, the manager of Boots' chemist, nurses from local hospitals, and so on. But from this core group the seminars grew both in size and in content. They included a wide range of issues facing the Soho communities, and, over the four years that they ran, speakers included a very diverse range of people: from the marketing director of Smith, Kline and French (the manufacturers of 'purple hearts') to Pete Townshend of The Who, from the Chief Inspector of the Home Office Drugs Branch to Dr David Smith, founder of the Haight-Ashbury Free Clinic, from junkies and speed freaks to peers of the realm, from local Soho workers to the staff of prisons and borstals. The audiences were equally varied. The seminars were an undoubted success in creating a kind of university of the streets in which all were teachers and all were learners, and there was an atmosphere of equality, informality and commitment.

The developments at St Anne's were part of a whole mushrooming of voluntary agencies concerned with drug abuse after 1967. These agencies fell into three broad categories: those concerned with preventive work, those concerned with crisis provision, and those concerned with 'rehabilitation' and aftercare.

41

1. *Preventive Work*

It is hard to say whether prevention or aftercare is the more difficult. The central problem in prevention is that there is no known way to stop people, young or old, from taking drugs. To prevent western young people, who have grown up in a drug-taking culture, from experimenting with drugs is simply not possible. When we use the word 'prevention', we are wise to use it in its older meaning, derived from the Latin, of 'going before'. We need to discover the most constructive and sensible ways of preparing the way for young people to grow up safely, and to behave wisely, in a world in which drugs are increasingly available. The best form of prevention is long-term care and support. The lessons of history are clear in at least one area: all the great diseases have been reduced by changes in the environment more than by the use of medicines or by crisis action. In the same way the most effective approach to 'prevention' in the area of drug use is the creation of a safe, warm, loving, environment in which communication is possible, the worth of the person is recognised, and support and help are always available. If conditions are hopeful, drug abuse is unlikely to develop or, if it does, it is unlikely to become serious. If not, no amount of 'drug education' will be effective. Indeed some would argue that drug-specific campaigns may have the opposite effect to the one intended.

While the family is of critical importance in the work of prevention, there are community aspects and agencies within most areas which can be helpful. One group with which I have been involved since the 1960s is a detached youth work project in the East End of London called Avenues Unlimited. Supported by the Young Women's Christian Association, Avenues has, for over twenty years, been one of the major youth work agencies concerned with drug problems in East London. Today I chair a drug prevention project which has grown out of the work done by Derek Cox and others over many years.

In the mid-1960s some youth workers associated with

Avenues tried to identify types of young people who were most at risk in relation to drug abuse. They identified three main types: the adolescent from a socially deprived neighbourhood who had left school at fifteen and become a member of a highly delinquent and disorganised group; the alienated adolescent from the suburbs; and the adolescent who had drifted into the large city and had no roots. In the East End context it was the first type with which we were – and still are – principally concerned. The workers compiled a list of about twenty young men and two young women who, they believed, were in danger of becoming addicted. The prediction was based on the fact that they were members of a delinquent culture, were regular users of certain cafes in the area, and had been seen regularly in the company of known drug addicts. In all cases the prediction was 100 per cent correct. But the workers felt that by the prediction stage effective preventive work was impossible, and they stressed the importance of working with a much younger age group since the social causes of drug abuse had built up over a very long period.

The youth and community worker is often in a strong position, in association with other agencies and individuals, to help both children and parents. In some areas multidisciplinary teams have formed on the lines pioneered by the Soho Drugs Group in the 1960s.

2. Crisis Work

In a report on our work in Soho in 1968 I wrote:

The role of Soho in the drug scene is primarily that of an area of infection. This observation is true at two levels. The adolescents on the 'pep pill fringe' in many cases use clubs and other centres in Soho as sources of supply, while heroin addicts still, though to a lesser extent than in earlier years, rely on the West End illicit market as a supplementary pool for additional supplies. Pastoral work on the drug scene in Soho possesses, because of this, two built-in limitations. First, it cannot be truly preventative, since the young people who have penetrated as far as the Soho scene are in many cases already badly damaged: the fact that they are in Soho at all means that they have passed the red light. Secondly, it cannot be rehabilitative, since to attempt rehabilitation within the area of infection would be self-defeating.[16]

Our work in Soho was essentially crisis work. In our contacts with drug takers, we aimed to be supportive, helping them to ensure that their 'Soho journey' was less destructive and harmful than it might be, and interventive, coping with overdoses, feeding, dealing with abscesses, and so on. We often provided a link at a critical stage between the life of the streets and long-term recovery and rebuilding. One of the most important pastoral lessons which I had to learn was that a casual contact made at 4 a.m. may have repercussions many years later. The casual contact must never be despised or underrated. In all crisis work, we are involved in the pastoral strategy of the long haul.

Contact with the street addict is often the initial stage in 'treatment'. The work of the Rink Project in Soho showed the long-term importance of street work and crisis support. The closing of this project by the Salvation Army, its sponsors, is one of the most tragic episodes in post-war urban Christianity. The Army could not comprehend or tolerate an approach which was not simplistically evangelistic, and the gulf between the Army hierarchy and their own street workers became unbridgeable. Arising out of a different context, the Simon Community was formed in 1963 with the aim of working at 'skid row' level with vagrant alcoholics and methylated spirit drinkers. But Simon workers also had close links with heroin addicts. Of all the 1960s projects, it was Simon which most clearly expressed the crisis dimension. As their founder put it in 1968:

Simon does not seek to rehabilitate but to *contain*. Its aim is to accept, assimilate, and then sort out. . . Simon workers, however, should not fall into the trap of aiming to restore to an unsympathetic society the men and women who, over and over again, have failed most, if not all, formal attempts to cure them.[17]

The Simon Community aimed to eliminate the 'us and them' syndrome, and their houses were closely modelled on those of the Catholic Worker. The kitchen was the focal point, and, as in the ministry of Jesus, the sharing of a common meal was the heart of their life and practice.

It is easy to exaggerate the difference between the situation in Soho and that in the majority of areas in the rest of Britain. Of course, Soho is different insofar as it is not a major residential district. Most of the young people come from elsewhere, and they have already passed a certain danger point before they arrive. Yet it became very clear from conversations with hundreds of young people in the clubs that one principal reason why they had left their home area was that they could not talk through their problems with anyone, least of all with their family. Their picture of the clergy and the church in general was not impressive. Indeed the church seemed to epitomise all that was unsatisfactory in society: its complacency, lukewarmness, and general unawareness of what was going on. Yet the kind of supportive care which we tried to provide was even more necessary in the areas from which the young people had come. Had it been available, they would probably never have arrived on our doorstep at all.

3. Aftercare Work

One of the really difficult problems in aftercare work is the fact that, in spite of its dangers, its violence, and its cruelty, there are aspects of the life of Soho and similar districts which are very accepting of deviance. People would feel accepted, absorbed into the Soho subcultures, in a way which contrasted with the narrowness and lack of acceptance which they had found in their home environments. To suggest a return to the very environment whose lack of understanding and compassion had been an integral part of the initial crisis was not the most helpful idea. Yet so much of the advice given to young people is based on such a 'return philosophy'.

People who have become very heavily involved with chemicals, often as alternatives to and substitutes for relationships with people, need years in which to rebuild their personalities and their relationships with society. Addiction provides an identity. To be a junkie is at least a status. As one addict wrote to me:

It's sad that they have to go this far to get help. I think 'help' is what they want rather than attention. After all, if you wear weird enough clothes you'll get attention. I used to want help but I couldn't say so. I only got it when I became a junkie.

The same person later told me that while she was an addict she knew that there would be social workers, doctors, nurses and others who would fuss around her: once she 'came off', everybody lost interest. Now she was just like everyone else – of no importance. Addiction at least provided an identity. The addict community offered a lifestyle within a climate in which the very notion of 'community' had become virtually meaningless.

If mainstream society offers no hope, no future, no understanding, it is hardly surprising that many people who have 'opted out' have no wish to return. Moreover, if society itself has become more destructive and deranged, how can one expect a destructive and deranged personal lifestyle to be abandoned? Much theorising about drugs assumes the existence of some kind of social norm from which the user has deviated and to which he or she can return. But there is no such norm. It is the non-drug user who is deviant in a culture where the use of mind-altering chemicals is endemic. In a drug-oriented society 'rehabilitation' may itself be a form of social deviance. In a non-caring society the recovery of care will necessarily involve conflict.

Speed kills: amphetamine and the spread of the needle culture

In both San Francisco and London it was amphetamine, particularly in the form of intravenous methylamphetamine hydrochloride (Methedrine), which transformed the character of the drug culture. The new population which took over Haight-Ashbury after 1968 were 'speed freaks', high-dose amphetamine users, and they created one of the most serious health problems in the city. The spread of methylamphetamine, used intravenously, transformed the peaceful hippy colony into a society of violent, psychopathic amphetamine users.

Soho in 1968 saw an epidemic of the intravenous use of Methedrine. However, unlike the American pattern which involved illicit speed labs, it is possible to show the precise pharmaceutical and medical sources of the drugs which constituted the London market, and to describe the demography and the pattern of distribution. This epidemic provided the fatal link between the needle addicts around Piccadilly and the pill users further north in the all-night clubs. Prior to 1968 there were two distinct communities of drug takers in the Soho area: the small community of heroin and cocaine addicts, junkies, injecting drugs; and a much larger community of many thousands of young teenage pill takers. For the most part, they did not meet. The spread of intravenous methylamphetamine brought them together.

There were two phases of amphetamine abuse in Soho. Before the Methedrine epidemic the Soho clubs constituted a conventional pill-taking drug scene. The years 1962–63 were a peak period for the use of Drinamyl, a combination of dexamphetamine and amylobarbitone, which became known as 'purple heart' (though it was in fact blue and triangular). Later addicts would look back on these years as the 'good old days' when the big discos contained thousands of pills. But after about 1965 the era of the big discos gave way to a period when, as many young people left Soho altogether, the drug traffic moved increasingly into the smaller clubs, coffee

47

bars and arcades. What happened in this period is well described by a youth worker, writing in 1969:

> Since 1963–4, the time of The Discotheque in Wardour Street and the rush of clubs run by Nash; the time of pep pill parties in the Leicester Square conveniences – when for a moment innocent girls and boys felt they had latched on to something really *new* – the word has come back – the West End's had it. Certainly the action in the last two or three years has been much more on the perimeter of London: a whole club-going sector of the youth of inner London turned their backs on the pathetic con of Soho and the West End and it's doubtful if they will ever need to come back.[18]

There were several sets of forces at work in these years. There was the movement of many young people away from Soho altogether, coinciding with the decentralisation of the amphetamine traffic itself (though heroin and its associated drugs remained more concentrated in London until the end of the decade). In Soho itself the community of injecting addicts grew rapidly, as it did in other towns which depended on London as a source of supply; while the increased concentration of the high-dose amphetamine users, now becoming more and more a part of the needle culture, in the smaller clubs led to the diversification and geographical spread of addiction. From the point at which Methedrine replaced cocaine as the injectable stimulant to be used alongside heroin, largely through the prescribing of Dr John Petro in the West End and Dr Christopher Swan in Hackney, the old divide between heroin addicts and pill takers had become very blurred. (See Appendix 2.)

A critical aspect of the spread of intravenous amphetamine was the centrality of the needle in the drug culture. Studies in the USA and in Britain have stressed that the process of injection is in many ways as important as the pharmacological properties of the drug. Increasingly, among the drug takers we were seeing after 1968, the really important line of demarcation was not between 'soft' and 'hard' drugs, which had always been one of the more misleading pieces of terminology, but between oral and intravenous drug use. The post–1968 needle culture did not involve only heroin but Methedrine, Ritalin, amphetamine sulphate powder, barbiturates, and a whole range of adulterated materials. By the early 70s the term 'polydrug use' was widespread.

While the view that all injecting users are bound for a life of permanent addiction is clearly false, my experience has been that once a person has entered the needle culture, he or she has entered a very destructive, and potentially a totally consuming, lifestyle. The needle and the ritual of injection take over and dominate the person's entire life so powerfully that only an experience of greater transforming power, such as falling in love or religious commitment, is likely to change it. The needle culture is a culture of despair, the ultimate negation of life. Yet it is essential to realise that people do not simply drift into addiction. The life of the addict is one which is deliberately chosen, it is a real choice which demands commitment and discipline. 'Junk is not a kick. Junk is a way of life'.[19] Williams Burroughs' words are reflected in the key line from the song 'Heroin', made by the rock group Velvet Underground: 'I have made a decision. I am going to try to nullify my life'. In the 60s it was common to interpret such an option in terms of personal pathology, family disturbance, immature personalities, and so on. The really dramatic and frightening shift since the 60s has been the shift from localised subcultures of mainly middle-class dropouts in London to a situation where whole regions – Merseyside, Glasgow, Dublin – have become heroin centres. The new addicts are very different: ordinary working-class young people, victims of long-term unemployment and social hopelessness.

Personal and political

In our ministry among drug takers in Soho, there were many areas where personal care became inseparable from political conflict. We found that government, funding bodies and sup-

49

portive individuals would be only too happy to commend and even finance the former, but would strongly resist and oppose any concern with the latter. The memorable words of Helder Camara, the Brazilian archbishop, often came to our minds. 'If I feed the hungry, they call me a saint. If I ask why they are hungry, they call me a communist'. Yet we could not merely minister at the individual level without being led to question the wider social, economic and political background. Three areas stand out in particular.

The first was in relation to the pharmaceutical industry. Most of the substances which caused concern, and which appeared on the Soho street market, did not originate in criminal syndicates or illicit street labs: they were manufactured by reputable pharmaceutical companies and arrived on the illicit market through prescriptions, thefts from warehouses and chemists' shops. The ethics of the pharmaceutical industry leave much to be desired. Many products have been promoted by advertising techniques which make pretentious claims which independent research does not support, and ignore serious evidence of side-effects. Many drugs which are marketed have little therapeutic value. The amphetamines are a classic case. No pharmacologists in the 60s, apart from those employed by pharmaceutical companies, would have denied that these drugs were more dangerous than useful, that they were in fact therapeutically obsolete, apart from one or two rare or restricted conditions. Yet they continued to be manufactured and they flooded the adolescent market in clubs and bars all over Britain. The Drugs (Prevention of Misuse) Act of 1964 gave one police officer the power to arrest one teenager for possession of one Drinamyl tablet: it gave no power over manufacture, distribution or control. There were, and are, many examples where drugs are manufactured, promoted and prescribed with very slight attention to the social and cultural context, and the potential for their abuse and the consequent human damage.

The second area related to the government provision – or, more accurately, lack of provision – for treatment and management of heroin addiction. The changes in legislation in 1968 which reduced the power of general practitioners to prescribe heroin and cocaine for addicts created a situation which was ripe for exploitation by criminal groups. Those of us who were close to the street drug scene warned and warned of the danger of this policy, and our warnings were ignored. The Minister of Health, Kenneth Robinson, advised us to keep on with our good work and not to criticise the government: the 'reverend gentleman', he observed, ought to have learnt the maxim 'Do good by stealth'. (Presumably he thought it was in the Bible!)[20] The Ministry of Health's line was that the wicked overprescribing junkies' doctors were responsible for the situation: but at the same time they hoped that these same doctors would continue to prop up the system until the government was ready with its new treatment centres, and would then gracefully withdraw. When Lady Frankau died, without advising the Ministry of her intention, she provoked the crisis which led to the escalation of the problem. Within months of the 1968 legislation, illicit powder heroin had appeared in Britain. Today the bulk of the heroin comes from criminal syndicates in Hong Kong, Iran and Pakistan. The clear warnings of danger ahead were unheeded and we have reaped the whirlwind. A combination of restrictive legislation on the one hand, and a failure to take seriously the need for care and treatment facilities on the other, has led Britain towards an American style situation. We have, as in so many areas, followed the United States at the very point at which all the evidence shows its policy to have failed conspicuously.

How could one care for individual addicts without pointing to the structural factors which made their own plight and the prospects for the future so much worse?

The third area was as wide as society itself, and yet could not be bypassed. For decades our society has encouraged dependence on chemicals. 'Better living through chemistry' has expressed a central thesis of our culture: that internal needs can be met, and internal problems can be solved, by the ingestion of the appropriate chemical. As a drug-taking society, we were in no position to be surprised or judgmental when young people also took centrally acting drugs to deal with their inner needs and problems. Young drug takers were seen as deviants, as rebels, as social outcasts. Yet nothing was so conventional, so central to the cultural conformities of western materialism, as drug use. The youth were doing what their parents had taught them. Indeed, throughout the period the 'typical British drug addict' was likely not to be a young person at all, but a middle-aged person dependent on alcohol, barbiturates, or the minor tranquillisers. Yet at the heart of this chemical culture there was appearing a new phenomenon, a movement of disaffiliation which is still working itself out.

The emergence of a new spirituality

It would be a major error to assume that the drug route of the late 60s led only towards despair and destruction: or to assume that all drug takers are motivated by the urge to self-destruction, the quest for 'kicks', or the need to escape or to kill pain. The motivations for drug use are immensely varied, and one central motivation which became increasingly clear after 1967 was the quest for spiritual experience, for transcendence, for the encounter with the divine.

'God in a Pill?' was the title of a pamphlet by the Indian guru Meher Baba which was circulated in San Francisco and Berkeley in 1966.[21] The idea seems on the surface absurd. Yet the use of mind-altering chemicals to increase apprehension of the divine has a long history: opium, the peyote cactus, magical mushrooms, cannabis (possibly the *soma* of ancient mythology) are among many substances which have been used for spiritual purposes since ancient times. In the modern period, Benjamin Paul Blood in 1874 and William James in 1902 used nitrous oxide as a route to mystical experience, while Aldous Huxley in the 1940s experimented with mescaline in his quest for 'the chemical conditions of transcendental experience'.[22] They were followed by Alan Watts and Timothy Leary in the 1960s with similar claims about psilocybin and LSD. It was Leary who located LSD use firmly within

52

a religious context as a sacramental substance. It was Leary who, in *The Psychedelic Experience*, made popular the notion of a drug-induced journey to new levels of consciousness. It was Leary who adapted the Tibetan Book of the Dead as a guiding text to the LSD experience.[23] Yet it was not until 1966 and 1967 that chemical-based spirituality became embodied in a mass cultural movement.[24]

LSD, however, long antedated the psychedelic culture of the late 60s. It was discovered by a Swiss scientist Hofmann in 1938, and was introduced to Britain at Powick Hospital, Worcestershire in 1954 as a psychotherapeutic agent. In the early days of LSD therapy, wildly extravagant claims were made for the drug which further research did not vindicate: it was seen as a 'royal road to the unconscious' and so on. Today few psychiatrists would stand by these claims, though one of those most faithful to LSD use, Frank Lake, founded the 'Clinical Theology' movement which aroused considerable support within the Church of England.[25] It is probable that a high proportion of those who experienced therapeutic LSD trips in these early years were Anglican clergymen. But by the time that the psychedelic culture developed, most psychiatrists had ceased to use the drug.

There are two ways of looking at the psychedelic movement. One is to say: these agents have led to profound spiritual experiences, comparable to those of the mystics (as well as psychotics). On this view the renewed interest in the spiritual quest is a direct result of the ingestion of psycho-active chemicals. To Leary the journey to new realms of consciousness involving transcendence of verbal concepts, of space-time dimensions, and of the ego or identity, was the heart of the psychedelic experience. He wrote:

> Such experiences of enlarged consciousness can occur in a variety of ways: sensory deprivation, yoga exercises, disciplined meditation, religious or aesthetic ecstasies, or spontaneously. Most recently they have become available to anyone through the ingestion of psychedelic drugs such as LSD, psilocybin, mescaline, DMT, etc.[26]

On this view, LSD stands in a similar position to that of the car or the telescope. It is perfectly possible to travel through the country by foot, and to study the stars by use of the naked eye, but it would be silly to do so. Similarly it is silly to pursue the road of mystical enlightenment without the use of those chemicals which have been made available to help us.

The second approach is to say: the renewal of the spiritual quest was inevitable as disillusionment with consumerism set in. When it came, it was not surprising that it became sidetracked for a while into the characteristically western route of drugs. On this view, the psychedelic culture was not to be seen as an alien growth but rather as the logical end of one facet of the dominant culture. As Theodore Roszak wrote:

> The gadget happy American has always been a figure of fun because of his facile assumption that there exists a technological solution to every human problem. It only took the great psychedelic crusade to perfect the absurdity by proclaiming that personal salvation and the social revolution can be packed into a capsule.[27]

So as the pharmaceutical industry offered hypnotics and tranquillisers for treatment of sleeplessness and anxiety, Leary offered psilocybin and LSD to treat spiritual sickness. Leary and his colleagues were the exact opposite to the ideology of Dr William Sargent of St Thomas's Hospital. Sargent, the high priest of chlorpromazine (Largactil), had claimed that 'under chlorpromazine a patient should be more immune to the spell of the witch doctor and probably to the religious revivalist as well.'[28] According to the pharmacology textbooks, the antidote to LSD was chlorpromazine.

I will discuss the spiritual ferment of the 1960s more in Chapter 3. Here I want merely to make the point that a good deal of contemporary drug use has been marked by a desire for transcendence, a search for meaning, and sometimes explicitly a search for God. It was clear as early as 1963 that the psychedelic movement was taking a spiritual direction. It was inevitable, because people were experiencing levels of consciousness which they could not explain in terms of their conventional medical and psychological models, and they were realising that the states which they experienced on LSD were closely similar to those described in the records of mysticism. But by 1966 some of the early disciples of the LSD cult were questioning the validity of the psychedelic claims. Prominent among them was Allan Y. Cohen, one of Leary's colleagues in his early drug research at Harvard. Cohen did not question the ability of LSD to bring about a religious experience. 'If I stick you in a church and give you 500 microgrammes of LSD, I will guarantee you a religious experience', he said in a seminar at St Anne's, Soho, in 1968. (He added, 'It might be of hell – but that's religious!') But Cohen questioned the relevance of the experience to the growth of religious life and the pursuit of spirituality. He claimed that reliance on chemicals could not help the development of true spirituality, and his critique centred on the nature of love.

> You can't carry over even the profound experiences you have. You can feel very loving under LSD, but can you exert that love to someone whom previously you didn't like? The long-range answer is no. It is almost beyond controversy. The controversy has now shifted into: maybe it can get you started, but something else has to end it – one's own effort. But when you see the psychedelic leaders of the world, after a gorgeously mystical brotherhood love session, as they are coming down, having a bitter argument about who should wash the dishes, a sense passes through one that somehow sainthood has been missed.[29]

In fact, in my experience, most of these LSD seekers moved from drugs towards non-chemical approaches to consciousness and to life.

Undoubtedly, for many young people, experience with LSD was a very positive one. It opened up their minds and hearts to new vistas of experience, and their subsequent lives have been enriched. Yet my overwhelming sense, as a result of experience of chronic drug users over a long period, is not one of hopefulness. I experienced a world of deep gloom and meaninglessness, of helplessness and the urge to self-destruction. I felt anger at the lack of concern so long as users are few or poor, and the marked change when children of cabinet ministers or the intelligentsia get involved. I experienced an acute feeling of boredom at the endless conversations about 'scripts', potency of drugs, overdoses, and related drug issues, and at the 'amotivational syndrome' which erodes interest in anything other than the drug and one's relationship with it. I have not experienced the drug culture as a zone of liberation. Ministering within it, I have at times felt engulfed in darkness and perplexity.

Increasingly the drug scene has come to be a symbolic representation of the character of our society. In the 1960s we were faced with large numbers of affluent youngsters who indulged in the products of consumerism, and a smaller group of tragic, isolated figures for whom heroin was a way to kill physical and emotional pain. Today we are faced with whole communities of despair who have discovered heroin as a drug which reflects and embodies their condition. It is the drug of the ruins, and the work of reconstruction, when these terrible years are over, will be very demanding.

Yet these years in which the drug culture was my world were years in which I learnt more about the inner meaning of Christian priesthood than at any other single period.

The drug culture and the character of priesthood

I believe that my experience of ministry in the drug culture illuminated the character of Christian priesthood in five major areas.

1. The eucharistic mystery

The four liturgical phases of the eucharistic liturgy – offertory, consecration, fraction and communion – acquired new and profound significance in the context of the drug culture. Not only did such worship itself become more important as I

56

recognised my own solidarity with the Body of Christ elsewhere. But the realisation of the eucharistic shape of all life and ministry came home to me with great force.

I came to see its materiality. If bread and wine, the fruits of the earth, the products of the industrial process, are brought within a redemptive climate, then surely we need to see that other fruits of the earth are not irredeemable. Cannabis, which botanically stands between the hop and the stinging nettle; LSD which derives from ergot which grows on rye wheat; heroin, the fruit of the opium poppy; can we say that these 'fruits of the earth and work of human hands' are beyond redemption? It is essential to avoid the gnostic rejection of all matter as evil. Any theological approach to drug use needs to begin with the doctrine of the goodness of creation and of the fruits of the earth.

I came to see its potential for sanctification. The recognition that both people, however degraded and damaged, and substances, however misused, can be transformed, sanctified, and made into vehicles of the spirit, came home to me in Soho with great force.

I came to see the place of brokenness. The recognition that our life and ministry is fruitful by virtue of its brokenness came alive. A breaking process has to occur before we can truly flourish. Only by being broken can we be shared.

I came to see its common character. At the altar, and in life as a whole, there is a solidarity of prince and prostitute, of addict and archbishop, of respectable and reprobate.

2. Intercession

In the Epistle to the Hebrews, the priesthood of Christ is seen very largely in terms of his intercession. I suppose it was a combination of a sense of helplessness, inability to achieve any obvious result by the direct approach, and a sense of being constantly thrown back onto God's mercy, and God's subtle ways of working, which brought home to me the central place of intercessory prayer in all priestly ministry. I still do not know how intercession works. But the bringing of people and their needs, and holding them within the ongoing stream of prayerful activity, is, I am sure, the most valuable thing that we can ever do for others. My notebooks and journals going back to the early 60s are packed with names. Many of the faces are still very clear and vivid. Many others have gone. In the silence, it is not uncommon for certain people to surface with great vividness. I know I need to pray for them very specifically. Sometimes they reappear unexpectedly in strange places.

3. Contemplative prayer

Closely linked with the prayer of intercession is that of contemplation, of waiting on God in the darkness and the silence. Again it is significant that it was the very active, even frenzied, atmosphere of Soho which helped me to realise the need for a contemplative dimension at the heart of all Christian ministry. It was not just the need to survive, important as that was. There was a recognition that, if I spent my days and nights rushing around feverishly doing good to others, there was a danger that I would communicate to them nothing more than my own exhaustion and inner emptiness. But it was the realisation that the warfare of the spirit has to be fought at a very profound inner level; that if, as Julian of Norwich says, God is the Ground in which we stand, then the closer one comes to God the closer one will be drawn to others in their suffering and turmoil.

This sense of solidarity and communion of God and humankind helped me to see that the redemption of the world did not depend on me, and that, although time was not on my side, God is the Alpha and the Omega, and that to God belong times and seasons. It was in Soho, at the heart of the drug scene at its most violent and most hopeless point, that some words of Thomas Merton imprinted themselves on my heart with the intensity of wounds.

You just lie there, inert, helpless, alone, in the dark, and let yourself be crushed by the inscrutable tyranny of time. The plank bed becomes an altar and you lie there without trying to understand any longer in what sense you can be called a sacrifice. Outside in the world, where it is night, perhaps there is someone who suddenly sees that something he has done is terrible. He is most unexpectedly sorry and finds himself able to pray.[30]

4. Spiritual Direction

I found in ministering to drug users that the last thing they looked to me for was an alternative form of social work. Rather did they look, in some mysterious way, for a sense of spiritual direction. Indeed they seemed more aware of the 'spiritual dimension' than did most church people. Drugs had opened up a new way of looking at reality. The need now was for guides who could help people to make sense of those levels of consciousness which they had experienced on drugs, and to integrate them into ordinary life, and this meant moving beyond the drug and beyond the experience to the underlying need. Hence the popularity of Zen, Yoga, and Krishna Consciousness, and a whole variety of eastern spiritual disciplines. It was at this point, in Soho, that two things happened. First, some ex-drug users stumbled across texts such as *The Cloud of Unknowing*, Eckhart and St John of the Cross (sold at Watkins' shop in Cecil Court) and became aware of a mystical tradition within Christianity. Secondly, some of them went to Christian priests and pastors, and were amazed that they knew nothing about this tradition. The mystically-oriented hippies ('meta-hippies') encountered the church at its lowest mystical point and its most activist phase. By the time the church caught up, a whole generation had been lost.

5. Darkness and priesthood

Much drug use, and most intravenous drug use in particular, is rooted in hopelessness and despair, and pastoral ministry has to enter into and experience something of that despair. A crucial question for our spirituality is how much despair we can take on board, and here, perhaps more than at any other point, the inner heart of priesthood came home to me. A book which spoke to me at that time was Ulrich Simon's *A Theology of Auschwitz* in which he speaks of priesthood as 'the office which ritually, inwardly and ascetically shares the dying and rising of Christ'.[31] The priest is 'defined' not by function or skill but by the inner spirit of sacrifice. In this sense the essential character of Christian priesthood is conferred at baptism.

But for the addict it was the dying without the hope of rising which we found. I realised, confronted with the dying of so many of my friends, that 'he descended into hell' is a phrase of the creed with a profound meaning. To minister to addicted persons involves us in a descent into hell, carrying hope but content to stay there. Stephen Delft's song, written in Soho in the 60s, expresses something of this.

> They say you've gone to heaven,
> But I have heard them tell
> That before you went to heaven, Lord,
> You also went to hell.

The song continued to reflect on the experience of drugs.

> They say you were victorious
> Over hell and over death.
> We know the hell of heroin,
> The dying that is meth.

The church cannot bypass death and hell.

The same point is made in Bruce Kenrick's account of the East Harlem Protestant Parish in New York in the 60s.

And we must face the horror of addiction because it underlines the fact that the church must suffer and be crucified with those it seeks to serve; and that it must keep on being crucified even though the nails bite deep and the hope of resurrection is obscure.

Kenrick continues:

But then there are other friends also. And these, in a tragic sense, have followed Christ as well. Like him they have suffered and been crucified; they have, as it were, descended into hell. But although their companions in the parish share their torments, here their 'following' has ceased. For they have not risen again. At least not yet.[32]

3

Midnight Hour

Ministry and Darkness

The spiritual ferment of the 1960s

I was ordained in 1964, the year after John Robinson's *Honest to God* was published. At that time it was common for parish priests to come back to the theological colleges which had trained their new curates with the complaint that their new curate did not pray, regarded prayer and meditation and even the sacraments as escapist and pietist, and simply wanted to rush about being relevant. By 1971 when I was on the staff of a theological college, it was more common to find newly ordained curates coming back to the college saying, 'My vicar doesn't pray. How can I get it across to him that if I want time for silence, meditation, and so on, I am not some kind of spiritual freak?' A superficial explanation of this change is that the curates of the 60s had become the vicars of the 70s. But there was more to it than this. A real spiritual shift had occurred. It was not an even development. While the church as a whole was beginning to take 'spirituality' seriously, it was possible in 1973 to hold a major conference in Norwich to celebrate the 600th anniversary of Julian's *Revelations of Divine Love* and find that the Penguin edition of the book was out of print! Yet it was only a matter of time before the paperback book trade caught up with the shifts in consciousness which were taking place.

Between 1967 and the mid–70s a spiritual movement was occurring which, on the whole, bypassed the institutional church. It was fascinating to observe, and to be part of, this spiritual ferment from the periphery of the church, particularly fascinating from the vantage point of Soho. Some strange things were happening. At the very point that the Second Vatican Council was simplifying the liturgy, throwing out its old vestments, and when many were claiming that the 'mystery' of the Mass was being eroded; when many Christians, influenced by Robinson, Harvey Cox and others, were concerned with 'involvement' and 'relevance', the hippies were donning flamboyant vestments, burning incense, learning eastern chants, and reading the Yoga Sutras of Patanjali. Religion seemed to be on the increase everywhere except within the church. In 1967 a book appeared in which there were the following words.

> We live in a secular world. To adapt to this world the child abdicates its ecstasy. . . Having lost our experience of the spirit, we are expected to have faith. But this faith comes to be a belief in a reality which is not evident. There is a prophecy in Amos that there will be a time when there will be a famine in the land, not a famine for bread, nor a thirst for water, but of *hearing* the words of the Lord. That time has now come to pass. It is the present age.[1]

The author was R. D. Laing, a psychiatrist. Laing was writing during this period of the urgent need for priests and physicians who could guide seekers after transcendence. But where, he asked, could they be found?[2] Laing was writing as a mystic and a theologian when many theologians were writing as if they were psychiatrists. During these years too The Beatles made an LP based on the Tibetan Book of the Dead; while, as the Roman Church got rid of Latin, Paul Simon sang the Benedictus in Latin at the Flamingo Club in Soho. The white-haired ladies who had for many years been disciples of Meher Baba were baffled when they were joined by Pete Townshend of The Who and Ronnie Lane of The Small Faces. It was a strange time.

Broadly speaking, the spiritual movements of the 60s followed five main directions. First, there was a revival of Zen. Zen had been popular among the beatniks of the 50s, such as Ginsberg and Kerouac. The Zen revival was a natural development of a quest for self-awareness and self-transcendence in a non-theistic and post-acid atmosphere. Secondly, various Hindu and other Asian traditions reappeared in westernised form, such as Krishna Consciousness, where non-chemical techniques such as the chanting of mantras were used to attain 'God-consciousness'; westernised forms of Sufism; and a major upsurge of interest in Yoga. Thirdly, various eastern texts – such as the Tibetan Book of the Dead, and the I Ching – were revived as guidebooks both to drugs and to natural experiences of self-loss. Fourthly, there was a revival of astrology and the occult. It was very clear that many conventional middle-class young people, on entering the psychedelic culture, developed a magical system of belief. There was great stress on 'the age of Aquarius', flying saucers, and so on, while the resurgence of the Glastonbury myths, supported by the influential writings of John Michell, was a major factor in the emergence of an astrological messianism which saw the dawning of the new age within the context of the movements of the stars. Michell wrote in 1972:

It is thus apparent that the Holy City of St John's vision, whose outlines are also found in the sacred precinct of Glastonbury, is not an original product of the Christian revelation, but an image of eternal truth, recognised and adopted by the builders of Stonehenge as the foundation stone of their temple, the model of the cosmic order translated to earth. The records of sacred history suggest that the type of consciousness associated with gnosticism, and with those aspirations implied in the squared circle symbol of the Holy City, occurs most particularly at the time of transition from one Platonic month to another within the great year, when the influences by which human intelligence was first promoted are again active. St John's Revelation is the work of the early Piscean era; Stonehenge was built at about the beginning of Aries. It is therefore quite in accordance with what might be expected that the plan of the cosmic city should again become visible at the dawn of Aquarius.[3]

The fifth direction taken by the spiritual revival of the 1960s was that of the 'Jesus Movement' and the charismatic renewal. These movements were, in my experience, mainly middle-class and suburban, and did not affect most of the young people with whom I was involved. Nevertheless the reappearance of a Jesus culture at the end of the 1960s was an important factor of the decade.

The demand for spiritual direction

To many rational Christians this was all very confusing. Many saw it as the resurgence of the irrational and the absurd. Much of it was. Roszak spoke of 'the lumpen-occult version of Abbott and Costello meet Jehovah'.[4] To many evangelical Christians the whole eastern revival was demonic. The appearance at the end of the 60s of Jesus Freaks, Arthur Blessit, the Children of God, and a variety of fundamentalist Christian hippies, was in part a response to the new religious revival. Within ten years these groups had been replaced by more sinister figures such as Jimmy Swaggart, Jerry Falwell and Pat Robertson.

There was much confusion, much dabbling, much syncretism and a general lack of direction. The churches were perhaps at their least perceptive point. So it was to eastern teachers, and to western exponents of eastern disciplines such as Alan Watts, that the new searchers turned. There seemed to be two reasons for the popularity of eastern teachers. First, they seemed to speak authoritatively about God and God-consciousness, and this seemed to be rooted in direct experience. By contrast, Christian clergy seemed to refer back to reports of other people's experiences. Secondly, they offered techniques and methodologies by which union with God could be attained. 'Chant the Hare Krishna mantra and your life

65

will be sublime'. (No other combination of syllables would work.) Other groups offered their own methods.

Was this a case of salvation by technique? Yes, certainly. But many Christians had assumed that prayer somehow just happened. There was a contempt for basic instruction on posture, method, discipline of time and so on, things which earlier generations of Christian teachers took for granted as necessary parts of the spiritual environment. So many of the neglected elements in the Christian ascetical tradition – such as fasting, meditation, and silence – came back in a non-Christian form.

It is possible to exaggerate the significance of all this. In my book *Youthquake*, I was careful not to portray the entire youth scene as if it were involved in a consciously spiritual quest. This did not deter some reviewers from accusing me of precisely that error. Laurie Taylor, for example, pointed out that many of the trends which I had described were only really evident in the London area and even there only among relatively small groups of people. He added, 'Life in Burslem, Tadcaster and Crewe was not greatly affected'.[5] I had thought that I had stressed the limited nature of the movements which I had described. In spite of these reservations, it was clear that there was a widespread craving for a deeper spirituality, for the exploration of consciousness, for interiority; a dissatisfaction with, and a moral revulsion from, consumerism and technocracy; a spiritual quest which had been forced into unorthodox channels by the bourgeois complacency and the spiritual superficiality of the mainstream churches. It seemed to me equally clear that this quest was much more widespread than many people assumed. Indeed many of the themes of the counter-culture of the 60s have now been taken on board by 'mainstream' society.

My own experience was that the demand for spiritual direction came first from these non-Christian seekers. Within a few years there was to be a manifestation of a need for deeper spiritual roots among Christians of varying traditions. But it was non-Christians, or people on the fringes of the churches, who were my main concern in Soho. As a Christian priest, surrounded by people searching everywhere for spiritual experience, I was drawn into a ministry of spiritual direction without quite knowing what I was letting myself in for. Most of the people who came my way had had no serious connections with organised Christianity. But they were people who realised that spiritual growth in itself was not enough; indeed, that growth without careful cultivation could produce no livable environment, but only the deadly luxuriance of swamp or jungle. The seriousness and the genuineness of their spiritual quest threw me back on my own inadequate inner resources. I was faced with a situation which the classical spiritual writers had not envisaged, for these were people who did not attend public worship, did not receive the sacraments, and were not always sure that they believed in God. We were in a new context which called for new approaches and new vision. I became convinced that what was true of Soho would soon become true of most of Britain, and I am sure I was right.

The insights of Thomas Merton

Nothing characterised the late 1960s so much as a sense of upheaval, or travail, of a new world struggling to be born, and a sense that simply to regurgitate old nostrums from a former age would not do. Yet at the same time, there was a desperate and intense search for lost traditions, for roots, for a spiritual foundation to living. Neither the false security of the 'fundamentalist' nor the trendiness of the superficial follower of fashion was what the era needed. As a priest ministering at the heart of the drug culture, surrounded by a new breed of spiritual seekers, I felt myself placed in the heart of a profound spiritual conflict.

It was at this point that I discovered Thomas Merton. What attracted me to Merton was that he was not afraid to face perplexity and upheaval. He saw clearly that conflict lies at the heart of spiritual life and pastoral ministry. Merton spoke to me as no other writer had done. Some words from

67

his *Conjectures of a Guilty Bystander* became imprinted on my heart and, more than any other modern text, shaped my spiritual journey.

We too often forget that Christian faith is a principle of questioning and struggle before it becomes a principle of certitude and of peace. One has to doubt and reject everything in order to believe firmly in Christ, and after one has begun to believe, one's faith itself must be tested and purified. Christianity is not merely a set of foregone conclusions. The Christian mind is a mind that risks intolerable purifications, and sometimes, indeed very often, the risks turn out to be too great to be tolerated. Faith tends to be defeated by the burning presence of God in mystery, and seeks refuge from him, flying to comfortable social forms and safe conventions in which purification is no longer an inner battle but a matter of outward gesture.[6]

Here in the writings of this contemplative monk I found a genuine wrestling with the world which I had now entered: a post-Christian world of spiritual confusion, spiritual darkness, spiritual perplexity; a world in which east and west, contemplative and political activist, Christian and Marxist, were seeking, struggling, to meet; a world which seemed to have entered a corporate dark night of the soul. Merton spoke to my needs and has continued to do so in a powerful and unique way.

I can best summarise the impact of this profound and complex figure by focussing on four themes.

First, Merton was concerned with the unmasking of illusion, a phrase and a theme which recurs throughout his writings. He saw the primary task of spiritual direction to be the struggle against illusion and unreality. He recognised the dangers of religious devotion which strove merely to nurture and strengthen false securities and to preserve the believer in false comfort. The need to discriminate between true spirituality and false had come to seem to me a most urgent pastoral task. Only a religion and a spirituality which places the unmasking of illusion at its heart can survive the Marxist critique of religion as an opiate.

Secondly, Merton was concerned with discernment and with contemplative listening. His books *Contemplative Prayer* and *Contemplation in a World of Action* are among the spiritual classics of the 1960s. He believed that without that contemplative orientation, religion in the end was bound to become an opiate. But contemplation and action were inseparably linked. Contemplation is concerned with clarity of vision, with silent attention to God and to the voices of the world. Merton saw the monastic vocation as one of listening to the neglected voices of the world. In one of his poems, he wrote of contemplation as 'listening to the skies we cannot understand, planted like sentinels on the world's frontier'.[7]

Thirdly, Merton was concerned to find and to serve Christ in the poor and lowly. In Chapter 1 I wrote of marginality, a theme which was central to Merton's later writings. He saw the monk as a marginal figure, one who withdraws to the periphery of the world in order to take a critical stance towards the world and to deepen fundamental human experience.[8] Through his own commitment to the very marginal life of solitude and seclusion he was drawn towards, and felt a deep affinity with, other marginal and peripheral people and groups.

Finally, Merton was concerned with the spiritual roots of resistance. From his solitude and seclusion he seemed to have an uncanny perception into the turmoils and conflicts of America in the era of Vietnam, the nuclear arms build-up and racial uprisings. His writings on peace and violence, on technocracy, totalitarianism and dehumanising trends in western culture, on black power, and on the dangers of a right-wing Christian backlash, are marked by a profound sensitivity and clarity of understanding as well as by the need to build up a Christian movement of resistance to injustice which will survive and will have deep roots.

In all these areas, Merton articulated the needs of my own pastoral agenda both in Soho and beyond: the struggle against illusion of all kinds; the cultivation of a contemplative spirit;

the commitment to Christ in the poor and downtrodden; and the building up of a culture of resistance to oppression and injustice.

The creative power of darkness

At the heart of Merton's spirituality is the theme of creative darkness. Originally it was his recognition of the place of darkness in the spiritual life which drew me to him. For here was a deeply optimistic, hopeful, catholic humanist, deeply rooted in the apophatic theology of Gregory of Nyssa, *The Cloud of Unknowing*, and John of the Cross, not at all gloomy or morbid, yet who saw the positive and liberating power of darkness. I had been troubled for years by the gulf between academic theology and spirituality on the one hand, and between spirituality and justice on the other. It is important to refer briefly to these two areas.

The captivity and confinement of 'theology' within the culture of academia represents a serious distortion of what theology actually is. One of the earliest definitions of theology is that of Evagrius of Pontus: 'A theologian is one whose prayer is true'.[9] *Theologia* in its ancient eastern sense involves the transfiguration of the theologian. It is a spiritual experience, involving purity of heart, communion with God, and entry into the darkness of faith. Theology can only occur within the climate of prayer and contemplation. I believe that the separation between thought and prayer, between head and heart, between study and altar, has been comfortable and convenient but not transformative or pastorally useful, indeed it has been pastorally disastrous. Theology has come to be seen as a preparation for doing something else better, and this cleavage between academic theology and the pastoral and spiritual task has led to the widespread belief among lay people that theology (which is, of course, only for clergy) should be over and done with by the time of ordination. The major American study by David Schuller and his colleagues brings this out clearly.[10]

70

I want to propose the opposite view that the only hope for a pastoral approach which can minister to the kinds of interior struggle which I have outlined and which can connect with the spiritual ferment of our age lies in the unifying of theology, spirituality and the pastoral task, and there are three practical consequences of this approach. First, it recognises that theology is by its very nature mystical, contemplative and prayerful. Secondly, it recognises that theology is expressed in worship and therefore that the aim of worship is communion with God. Thirdly, it recognises that the contemplative path is common and open to all, it is not esoteric but ordinary.

If this is true, then the emphasis which is so fundamental not only in western spiritual teachers such as the author of *The Cloud of Unknowing* and John of the Cross, but also in earlier eastern apophatic theology, as expressed by Gregory of Nyssa, Pseudo-Dionysius and others, on the divine darkness, the way of *agnosia*, unknowing, needs to be seen as relating not only to the individual but to corporate life. It means rediscovering the mystery of God as the very centre of all our theology, all our worshipping life, and all our pastoral practice. At the heart of the mystery of God in the Judaeo-Christian tradition is the darkness of Sinai and of Calvary. There can be no rational, genteel, liberal route to God which bypasses that central darkness.

It is here that the teaching of St John of the Cross on the dark night is of critical importance. St John is often misunderstood in two ways. He is seen either as a diagnostician of spiritual pathology, the dark night is seen as a kind of illness, a synonym for depression or 'the blues', an experience of spiritual desolation through which we pass, and from which we recover, in a few days or weeks. Or he is seen as a spiritual guide for eccentric spiritual elites, the very pious, neurotic old nuns, or people at the top of the spiritual ladder.

But St John is not writing about pathology and the dark night is not an illness. He is describing that central dimension of darkness at the heart of the very life of faith. The dark night is in fact a synonym for the life of faith. It expresses his attitude towards the whole of reality.[11] The dark night is in

71

fact identical with the living flame of love, the light of God as experienced in finitude and obscure perplexity: the difference is the perspective from which it is experienced. To minds that are finite, infinite light appears as total darkness. St John is not writing for elites: the dark night has to be entered by all, though its shape and form will differ. For it is nothing less than the entire spiritual journey by which, through sharing the darkness of Christ's self-emptying, we are healed.

The dark night of the soul is a process of disillusionment, the undermining of the false self, and a return to our true centre in God, the ultimate ground of reality. It is a process of liberation through disillusionment. The attainment of spiritual freedom is its goal. There is a unique quality in darkness. It is a unique source of insight and a unique climate of spiritual maturity. As St John points out, in the spiritual journey we travel fastest at night. The dark night is not the same as despair or disintegration, though these often accompany it. We go to pieces as a necessary part of the movement of transformation. What disintegrates is not our true self but the defences which surround it. We come to the end of our 'know how' in order to enter the darkness in which God is known. Spiritual direction aims to help people enter this darkness, moving away from their artificial lights and false securities.

If the encounter with darkness lies at the core of contemplative spirituality, its fruit is silence. The images of watching and waiting dominate the literature of the contemplative life: vision and attention, the ministry of eyes and ears, and linked with them in the experience of contemplation in the world of action are the images of which I have written earlier – those of helplessness, marginality, bafflement. These images are brought together in Merton's poem 'The Quickening of John the Baptist'.

Night is our diocese and silence is our ministry.
Poverty our charity, and helplessness our tongue-tied
    sermon.
Beyond the scope of sight and sound we dwell upon the
    air,

Seeking the world's gain in an unthinkable experience.
We are exiles at the far end of solitude, living as listeners,
With hearts attending to the skies we cannot understand,
Waiting upon the first far drums of Christ the Conqueror,
Planted like sentinels on the world's frontier.[12]

Night, helplessness, the tongue-tied sermon, exile, the skies
we cannot understand: these are not the qualities which dioceses look for in their clergy. They want daybreak people,
well-prepared sermons, and men and women who are in control of their material.

Yet, as Merton wrote in 1953, 'if preaching is not born in
silence, it is a waste of time'.[13] A pastoral ministry which is
not rooted in contemplative vision and attention, rooted in
darkness and waiting on God, will be superficial and potentially damaging to those who are its recipients and perhaps
its victims. The person who tries to act for others but does
not deepen self-understanding, freedom, integrity and the
capacity to love in his or her own heart, has nothing to give
but obsessions and delusions. Only those who have practised
silence in darkness can be true pastors.

A corporate dark night

One of my predecessors at St Anne's, Soho, was Father Gilbert Shaw. He was one of the most valued spiritual directors
of his day, a contemplative pastoral activist, and after he left
Soho he became Warden of the Sisters of the Love of God, a
contemplative order based in Oxford. He died in 1967, the
year in which I moved to Soho. In his papers he often referred
to a 'corporate dark night' which he believed was coming
upon the church. In one paper he wrote:

> It is vital that we should understand the changes of our
> age, and we can only do so if our prayer goes deep enough
> to root us in the unchangeability of God. If our eyes are
> fixed on him, then, however violent the changes, we are
> not limited by ideas conditioned by the past or the present.

73

We can help the present age by asking the right questions to enable people to see their need, and by standing firm in the stability of prayer to bring in God's true purpose. . . In this confidence we can face the night that has come upon the church, knowing it has a purpose of purification, a purification necessary for bringing us back to root principles.[14]

Like Shaw, I believe that we are in a situation in which the shaking of the foundations is no longer an individual, interior shaking: we are faced with the disintegration of the foundations of our society, with a 'dark night of our institutions',[15] a corporate dark night. St John of the Cross and the Carmelite tradition paid little attention to the social and political context within which spiritual darkness and upheaval occurred. The interior journey, the ascent of the soul to God, with all its turmoil and turbulence, took place within the sure and secure stronghold of the church and is sacraments, and the church itself, in spite of the upheavals of the Reformation, was at least at the heart of the culture of Spain.

Today none of these things can be assumed, in Britain or anywhere else in the western world. Both the churches and the western democracies, the whole capitalist order and the cultural context of its life, are in crisis. This can be very frightening or it can be full of hope (combined with uncertainty and obscurity as hope always is.) As long as we identify Christian faith and life with the values of dominant cultures, the collapse of one will be synonymous with the collapse of the other. The danger is crudely evident in the powerful campaigns of the New Christian Right in the United States, both in its crude electronic form, and in its more academic forms, but it is not entirely absent from the writings of Archbishop Habgood, the theology of *Faith in the City* and other Anglican reports. There is a widespread assumption that the church is a focal point for the unity of the nation, that there is a body of shared values, moral norms, principles of compassion and care, common to church, government and people.

I believe that this is increasingly false, and dangerous as a basis of action.

Any theological or pastoral strategy which is based on illusion can only foster and perpetuate further illusion, and much of our ecclesiastical life is rooted in illusion or at least is ambivalent. So bishops often address the nation as if they were spokesmen of the national religion (as indeed they are in law) rather than spokesmen of one minority among others (as they are in fact). One of the aims of the dark night, according to St John, is to purge us of illusion, falsehood and unreality, and this is painful. I believe that the process needs to take place not only at the personal but also at the institutional level.

When I was a teenager in the 1950s it was the thinking and friendship of the philosopher Alasdair MacIntyre which, more than any other single influence, led me to take Christianity with intellectual seriousness. In some respects, MacIntyre's analysis of contemporary western muddles and incoherence in his recent books *After Virtue* and *Whose Justice? Which Rationality?*[16] is a development of ideas which he was proposing in the 1950s. Thus in 1956 he spoke of the 'loss of any overall sense of significance in western society'. The 'combination of liberal morality and metaphysical meaninglessness' was, he argued, the central characteristic of our culture. Because of this we were at the prey of 'any passing evangelist of unreason who will promise a coherent view of the world and a coherent programme for changing it.'[17] From MacIntyre's present vantage point in the USA he is in a strong position to see how precisely and depressingly his warning has been fulfilled in the recent powerful upsurge of irrational versions of Christianity which seek to capture the 'naked public square'.[18] Yet, in spite of their efforts, the public square remains naked. Between the individual and the state there is nothing. Religion, which once played a central public role, is now increasingly marginalised to the realm of individual morality.

The central argument of *After Virtue* was that western society lacked any shared moral and spiritual values, and that the sooner this was recognised the more likely we would be to base our thinking and actions on realism and not on illusion. MacIntyre went on to argue that we had entered a new dark age, though, unlike the first dark age, the barbarians were not on the frontier but in our midst, and had been ruling us for some time. The most urgent immediate task, he claimed, was the 'reconstruction of local forms of community', a 'network of small groups of friends', within which moral and spiritual values could be preserved through 'the coming ages of barbarism and darkness', 'the new Dark Ages which are already upon us'. We were waiting, he concluded, for a new, no doubt very different, St Benedict.[19]

The renewal of the contemplative tradition

What does MacIntyre's analysis, contained in two major works published in the 1980s, mean for the contemporary practice of the Christian life? Let me identify four features of Christian spirituality which seem to be crucial if we take his thinking seriously. First, Christian spirituality must be rooted in what Stanley Hauerwas terms a 'community of character', a counter-society which, through its life and practice, can offer a 'contrasting model' to that of the dominant society.[20] Hauerwas's thinking on social ethics has paralleled Mac-Intyre's very closely.

The development and working out of what this means in practical terms within the British context is a major task for Christians. It is not enough to 'wait for a new St Benedict' as MacIntyre suggests: the urgent task is to recognise and cooperate with those networks which are already, in fragmentary and stumbling ways, forming a culture of resistance to the present barbarism. It is out of such networks that new forms of community, new models of what it is to be the church in the world, will emerge. For what the church is in its life carries more meaning than what it says. It is out of this recognition that something similar to the 'confessing church' of the Nazi period may well emerge.

Secondly, the Christian life must be rooted in the continuity of tradition. Rootless liberalism is no adequate basis for spiritual growth or for radical commitment. Authentic spirituality is never a 'flight of the alone to the alone' but is a corporate discipline of a community of memory and transforming history. The Christian life specifically is one which is lived within the 'subversive memory', the *anamnesis*, of the life, death and resurrection of Jesus of Nazareth. That memory is central to the eucharistic *anamnesis*, the heart of all Christian worship. The German theologian J. B. Metz stresses the need of 'anamnetic solidarity', solidarity in memory, with the event of Jesus.[21] The individualism which is so central to liberalism is in stark contrast and conflict with the Christian idea of the body of Christ, the organism of a new humanity.

So it is that a major part of Christian renewal, now as in Bonhoeffer's Germany, must lie in the reconstruction of the concept of the community of discipline, rooted in the tradition of prayer and struggle. Nicholas Lash, reflecting on MacIntyre in his study *Theology on the Road to Emmaus*, claims that

> a not unimportant responsiblity for the future of humanity could be exercised by a transcultural, global 'network' of local communities, each of which conceived its primary duty to be that of sustaining, in its particular place, the memory of him in whose dying we discern the transformative presence of God; communities which, in that act and process of remembrance, sustain an absolute hope for all humanity in the light of which to stimulate resistance to those dreams and nightmares in which individual nations and destinies, individual projects and policies, are destructively idolized.[22]

Thirdly, there must be a recognition that the tradition is alive and dynamic. Many today who call themselves, or who are called 'traditionalists' are effectively ignorant of the tradition, and are merely reactionary, backward, rigid and frightened. Living traditions embody conflicts and areas of growth and divergence, and when people start to dig into the tradition they find many surprising and threatening things. The tradition contains subversive dimensions, areas of contradiction and paradox. It is not a closed system but a liberating tradition which contains the seeds of further developments and opens up new paths for new journeys of faith. Thus liberation theology is both building upon a profound rebel tradition going back to the Jewish prophets, and yet is breaking new ground. Much of what passes for traditional Christianity in the west is no more than captivity to the past. Those who can only recognise the events of the past, and cannot discern the present or future, are the damned of Dante's vision. Yet we need to remember Marx's words: it is out of our old history that our new history will be made.

For, finally, the Christian vision is rooted in historical movement. We are witnessing, and are part of, the disintegration of our present order of society. 'Thatcherism' is only its current manifestation. Yet, if we are to believe the spiritual guides of Christian tradition, disintegration and death can be creative, the birth pangs of a new age, the corporate dark night of the soul which opens up new vistas of light. It is through death and descent into the chaos that resurrection comes. If we believe this, then the way forward for traditional Christians is not the way of conformity, the Constantinian option which has now ceased to be a moral option, nor the way of flight to the desert, important and valuable as that was in the fourth century, but the way of subversive orthodoxy, of creative maladjustment. For, as Martin Luther King once said:

> This hour in history needs a dedicated circle of transformed nonconformists. . . The saving of our world from pending doom will come not through the complacent adjustment of the conforming majority but through the creative maladjustment of a nonconforming minority.[23]

The politics of darkness

For St John of the Cross, the experience of darkness is marked by struggle and inner conflict. Without such conflict there can be no real progress. It is necessary, if we are to mature in the life of the spirit, to pass through 'some pretty rough and decidedly ugly country'.[24] The process is one of death and rebirth. The rebirth to true humanity is a painful one, and it may result in abiding wounds. In Marcel Legaut's words, 'these conversions to humanity bear the marks of violence and suffering linked to a difficult birth. Some deliveries result in scars that are often permanent'.[25] It is this process of death and rebirth which is St John's concern in his teaching about the dark night of the soul.

However, neither St John nor the Carmelite tradition as a whole develop the social consequences of this teaching or its implications for pastoral practice, though others have done so. J. B. Chautard, in his great work *The Soul of the Apostolate*, claimed that the success of the active apostolate was directly related to the numbers of Christians who had entered the illuminative way.[26] More recently the Chilean pastor Segundo Galilea has explored the symbols of desert and dark night in their relation to the encounter between mysticism and politics.[27] Galilea writes from a background of liberation theology which has begun to grapple with Marx. How might an encounter between Marx and John of the Cross help us to relate the spirituality of darkness to the politics of struggle?

First, it would help us to see that alienation, dehumanisation, oppression, are political and personal realities, and that political and personal are interlocked. Within the culture and value system of capitalism, relations between people are reduced to the level of things, in the subordination of all reality to the market. The identification of the forces which contribute to alienation, which destroy humanity and oppress individuals and groups, needs to be a central focus of contemplative reflection, and is vital if our pastoral activity is not to be detached from the concrete reality of our society. Human beings make history, but they do not make it just as they please. As Marx stressed, it is out of our old history that our new history is made. In theological terms, in dealing with these forces, we are confronting sin, and sin works to break up the human family, to sap its initiative, to destroy its freedom. Christians need to take seriously the ways in which sin is manifested within the structures of particular societies if we are to play our part in the work of redemption.

The personal dimensions of struggle have been seriously neglected in Marxist and other secular socialist traditions as well as within much liberal political thinking. One of the major contributions of socialist feminism has been to question both the neglect of the personal in politics, and the rigidity of a political orthodoxy from which doubt and darkness are excluded. Within secular politics it is certainly true that 'women have thus far led the way in the attempt to integrate spiritual consciousness with popular radicalism'.[28] Sheila Rowbothan's essay in the symposium *Beyond the Fragments* must remain one of the key texts in the socialist *ascesis* of self-examination and scrutiny. Her description of some of her former comrades within organised Marxism could equally be a description of many church people. 'They had all those certainties as if everything was known, the whole world and its history was sewn up and neatly categorised'.[29] Rowbotham goes on to attack the neglect of personal feelings in the concern for 'transcendent correctness', and she particularly criticises the doctrine of the vanguard, the Leninist party – 'a red zone from which professional revolutionaries sally forth with a superior knowledge, untouched by culture themselves, to insert, inject, imbue, or saturate and drown other movements'.[30]

The scene of naive and doctrinaire arrogance which Rowbotham describes is precisely that from which the dark night is needed to deliver us. In recent years many Christians have come to see the place of the dark night and of the 'way of unknowing' at the personal level. Often they have been propelled into it by forces within them and without – a breakdown or some crisis which has caused them to rethink and revalue all their certainties and securities. They have had to go back and start all over again, and yet with a wisdom and a depth which only darkness and apparent disintegration could have brought. They have come to see that the first step in the knowledge of God is a 'deliberate act of unlearning'[31] and that a rigid commitment to certain 'orthodox' positions, a commitment from which the dimension of personal struggle has been suppressed, is a serious obstacle to spiritual progress. That is why self-abandonment and trust in the darkness of the path before us is so necessary. In Merton's words:

> It becomes overwhelmingly important for us to become detached from our everyday conception of ourselves as potential subjects for special and unique experiences, or as candidates for realization, attainment and fulfilment. In other words, this means that a spiritual guide worth his salt will conduct a ruthless campaign against all forms of delusion arising out of spiritual ambition and self-complacency which aim to establish the ego in spiritual glory. That is why St John of the Cross is so hostile to visions and ecstasies and all forms of 'special experience.' That is why the Zen masters say 'If you meet the Buddha, kill him'.[32]

But for the most part this way of unknowing has not been seen as necessary at the socio-political level. We have not seen its relevance to political struggles. Yet it is in the political arena more than anywhere that we see the domination of clichés, unexamined assumptions and doctrinaire positions which have ceased to connect with reality. It is the world of politics more than anywhere that desperately needs the disturbing questioning of darkness and dissent. In the 1960s we were helped by R. D. Laing to see that 'the condition of alienation, of being asleep, of being unconscious, of being out of one's mind, is the condition of the normal man'[33] Laing urged a rethinking of conventional notions of sanity and madness. But if we seek to relate the traditions of the dark night and of unknowing to the structures of society, it will involve a much more ruthless and widespread critique of established assumptions and values right across the board, and this is a task of prophetic urgency.

Like Marx, St John of the Cross believed that human beings were changed in the course and process of movement. The dark night is a process of movement and upheaval within the person. Marx saw revolution as a process of movement and upheaval outside the person, but one which makes significant changes in personal consciousness. For consciousness is shaped by events, being is shaped by action. The new humanity is brought about in the actual course of struggle, by throwing oneself into the movement. As in the dark night, one is, in a sense, out of control, swept along by a historical process. The familiar structures of our world are shaken. We are never the same again.

Much Christian writing seems to assume a highly rational view of human consciousness and of social change from which both the experience of internal upheaval and the struggles of political life have been removed. Much political strategy, on the other hand, is based on a view of consciousness as something injected into people, 'brought to the workers only from without',[34] brought to them by an enlightened vanguard or educated elite. It is precisely from this view of reality, whether religious or political, that the dark night is needed to deliver us. Real change does not occur in our heads or by diktat from above, but through the shaking of the foundations of self and society.

My experience has been that there is a central core of darkness and of 'unknowing' which lies at the heart of human struggle. The moment we lose contact with this dark core we are in danger of becoming inhuman, fanatical, zealots, or of retreating into a world of increasing unreality. Both zealotry and false pietism share a certain kind of militant clarity which is rooted in a diminished mode of consciousness. We are all in danger of this diminishment. Politics without spirituality is in danger of becoming a kind of terrorism, moral, intellectual or physical. Spirituality cut off from politics moves into unreality and fantasy. The unity of the two depends upon a recognition of the place of darkness in our personal and political life.

82

Darkness and light in pastoral care

I want to conclude this chapter by identifying some features of a pastoral style of ministry which takes seriously the tradition of contemplative prayer and of the dark night; and then point to some areas where I see problems, dilemmas, and major work needing to be done.

At the heart of a contemplative pastoral ministry is the practice of listening. We talk a lot about listening, but it often comes too late, when nothing can be done. Much of the life of our institutions is rooted in structural, systemic deafness. We listen with our ears but our subsequent responses show that we have not heard. A contemplative approach to ministry involves serious and prolonged listening, and this can only take place in the midst of a conversation – which means keeping all lines of communication open.

A contemplative ministry will be a ministry in which silence plays a major role. The eastern monks spoke of *hesychia*, inner stillness, the condition of the prayerful soul. St Gregory Nazianzen claimed that the essential characteristic of the theologian was inner calm, and he contrasted this with the breathlessness of the mad.[35] Pastoral care is in real trouble if it loses the silent dimension. It becomes breathless and mad. It collapses into excessive and increasingly superficial talk and noise, and loses the capacity to attend to the inarticulate and those who have been reduced to silence by the intensity of their suffering. Much silence is the result of suffering and hopelessness. Only a silence rooted in careful attention can begin to respond to it.

A pastoral ministry which has taken darkness to its heart will not be desperate for quick solutions, for tidy systems. It will recognise that many dilemmas and perplexities are not solved, but are rather lived through.

A contemplative pastoral ministry will be characterised by simplicity. This seems a contradiction for I have written much about complexity and bafflement. Yet there is a kind of simplicity, a purity of heart, which only comes as a result of profound inner conflict, and which enables us to dispense

83

with much of the overcrowding in our minds and lives, and so to focus more on the abiding realities.

A pastoral ministry which is rooted in contemplative awareness will not be concerned with the provision of comfort, but rather with the potential for change. For the way of darkness is the way of progress, the way of transformation.

One of the purposes of the dark night of the soul is to break down our false enclosures and securities, our protections against threats, and to set us free to hear and heed new things, new voices, to face up to very troubling and painful parts of ourselves and of the world. Let me suggest seven areas where much reflection and inner struggle, as well as corporate debate and dialogue, needs to be done. Each of them provides material for another book.

First, clericalism. There are two large problems here. There is the fact that much Christian spirituality is a spirituality for clerics, adapted for lay people, who are seen as second-class citizens within the church. Then there is the related problem that the clerical caste has created its own artificial and unreal world, its culture of illusion, which cuts the clergy off from any real encounter with the world.

Secondly, the position of women. While the debate about the ordination of women to the priesthood remains important, it can easily become a way of absorbing some women into the present male-dominated system and so controlling them. The much deeper problem is the inability of men to take seriously the issues raised by feminist thinking.

Thirdly, the question of faiths other than Christianity. There are now more Patels than Robinsons in the London telephone directory. How can Christian spirituality exist in a multi-faith society? How can we begin to learn from India and Africa? What has Merton to say to us on this? What about the Holocaust?

Fourthly, the issues raised by liberation theology in Latin America and elsewhere. It is all to easy – and disastrously mistaken – to add liberation theology as a subject to the existing theological agenda, and so to miss its essential meaning and message. If theology is not a theology of liberation, it is bound to be a theology of oppression. It cannot be neutral, a theology of nothing.

Fifthly, the question of black theology and black spirituality. Black Christianity is flourishing in British cities. Most practising Anglicans in many inner-city districts are black. But most 'mainstream' Christian writing ignores this dimension of reality. More and more it is rooted in illusion.

Sixthly, issues about sexuality. I am increasingly troubled by the deep fear of human passion and sexuality which seems so deeply rooted in the Christian church. If sexuality and sexual energy is the raw material of sanctity, why is it that the church seems to be the one place where serious debate on these issues is not possible? So much Christian discourse on sexuality is based in illusion.

Finally, the area of politics. Political discourse, like religious discourse, is riddled with clichés, slogans and 'fundamentalisms'. How can the contemplative and the political activist meet in a way which both guides and strengthens the struggle for justice and which takes seriously the dignity and integrity of the human person?

In all these areas, the dominance of the doctrinaire and the crusading mind, the fostering of illusion, and the resistance to new truth represent serious dangers for the future. If contemplative spirituality and the tradition of the dark night means anything in social terms, it must surely mean that the Christian community ceases to be a closed, rigid, fearful and prepackaged structure, and becomes an open, flexible, liberated and learning community, a community which is open to the future, ready for risks, ready for the revelation of new truths, ready to follow where the Spirit leads us.

4

The Mark of Cain

Ministry and Racial Justice

On the 4 May 1978 Altab Ali was murdered a few hundred yards from my house in Bethnal Green. The murder sparked off a series of demonstrations and protests by the Asian community in East London and nationally against both racial violence and the institutionalised racism of the state. The murder of Altab Ali was not an isolated incident. There had been a whole history of racially motivated attacks in the East End going back to the early 1970s. It was in 1969 that the term 'Paki-bashing' was first used on the Collingwood Estate in Bethnal Green. These early attacks occurred at a time when the racial climate nationally was deteriorating. Each major speech by Enoch Powell had been followed by violent incidents in East London and elsewhere. There had been other speeches and media coverage of race issues. Of course, such public figures were often quick to deny that any increase in violence was their intention: but, wittingly or not, they helped to create a climate in which racist abuse and violence became more acceptable in British society.

The years from 1970 to 1976 saw a steady increase in racial attacks in Bethnal Green, where I had become parish priest in 1974. St Matthew's Church stood on the divide between a Bangladeshi area to the south and a mainly white area to the north where, for over thirty years, fascist groups had been active. The main street of the district was Brick Lane. At one time the heart of the Huguenot silk weaving district, it had become the main street of the Jewish ghetto at the end of the nineteenth century. By 1976 it was the centre of what was later to become known as 'Banglatown'. A building on the corner of Brick Lane and Fournier Street symbolised the history: once a Huguenot church, it had become a synagogue in the nineteenth century, and is now a mosque.

By 1976 the Bangladeshi community numbered around 15,000. Most of the population had originated in the Sylhet region, particularly in three villages. The southern part of Brick Lane had become the focal point of the community. Meanwhile the National Front (NF), a racist political party which had been founded ten years earlier, had established its main London base to the north of Brick Lane. Graffiti announcing 'We are back' and 'Keep Britain White', accompanied by swastikas and other fascist insignia, appeared on walls in Bethnal Green. Every Sunday between 50 and 300 NF supporters would gather to sell literature and abuse passers by who were black, Asian, or Jewish, or looked as if they might be students, left-wing, homosexual, or anything which contradicted the stereotype of the typical British patriot – white, with short hair and large boots. Organised racism had returned to the East End and had established a secure base at St Matthew's parish.

Formed in 1966–67, the National Front was an uneasy fusion of three organisations representing distinct traditions: the League of Empire Loyalists, an old-fashioned Tory imperialist stream; the Racial Preservation Society, a vaguely Christian fundamentalist racist grouping with its base in Sussex; and the Greater Britain Movement, led by John Tyndall, an explicitly Nazi organisation. The new party made little progress from 1967 to 1972, partly because of the popularity of Enoch Powell in these years. But a strong base had been established in East London in the old white working-class districts where Mosley had been active in the 1930s. These districts were characterised by years of neglect, a loss of identity (Shoreditch and Bethnal Green, the smallest boroughs in London, had been absorbed into Hackney and Tower Hamlets in 1965), and a very reactionary Labour Party which had long since ceased to stand for any socialist principles. The Labour Party in Bethnal Green was deeply racist, very secure and utterly ineffective. The National Front gained most of its recruits from disillusioned members of the Labour Party.

However, the NF had also attracted a large community of very alienated, disenchanted young people, many of them having a long history of truancy, family pathology, delinquency and drug taking (though this had subsided in the 1970s), a community heavily involved in petty crime and vandalism. It was within this community that 'Paki-bashing' originally took root. The NF gave these young people an identity as no other group had done. In a climate of unemployment, with little hope for the future, and in an atmosphere of captivity within run-down and dehumanising estates, vandalism had become the last available form of social action. The coming of the NF into this situation marked the expansion of vandalism into a political movement.

By 1978 the racial situation in the East End was extremely dangerous. On the 11 June five hundred skinheads, recruited from Essex and Hertfordshire as well as East London, rampaged through Brick Lane, smashing windows and attacking any Bengalis in sight. This spectacle was repeated on several occasions. Further north, Bethnal Green had become unsafe for Asian people at any time. Anyone who drew attention to the position was certain to receive threatening phone calls, razor blades through the post, death threats, and so on.

So I found myself as parish priest of an area with one of the highest votes for the NF in Britain. 25 per cent of St Peter's Ward had voted for the NF in the Greater London Council elections of 1977.[1] Many parishioners were NF sympathisers, as were many of the stallholders in the market from whom I bought my vegetables. I recall the head of a local primary school, almost in tears, after witnessing children of seven marching into the playground shouting 'Sieg Heil! Sieg Heil!' At the height of the NF campaign, there was a sense of being engulfed by a presence of evil, and a sense of the urgency of taking a public position with all the consequences that such action might bring. Yet there was the problem of how racial violence and prejudice could be handled pastorally. Was a 'position' enough? Might it be the counter-productive, and lead only to the hardening of attitudes?

Clearly support for the victims was important, but this was easier said than done. Many Bangladeshi families were very suspicious of help offered by white people. The police were particularly suspect because of their inaction in the face of racial attacks, or the fact that, if and when they did respond, they often seemed more interested in the immigration status of the victim than in the identity of the perpetrators. More generally, the personal experience of white people was, in many cases, not good. White men with short hair and big boots were NF unless proved otherwise. I was often able to be accepted, partly because I had been around for a long time, and partly because many of the leaders of the emerging Bangladeshi youth movements were my friends. But the building up of trust was a slow process, and there were so many negative factors in the political climate working against it.

A more tricky problem was how one ministered pastorally to racists and the perpetrators or supporters of violence. What happened if one's critical and 'prophetic' role, one's fidelity to the gospel, undermined one's 'pastoral' role? To the Socialist Workers' Party, the answer was simple. Racism was to be dealt with by argument, sales of newspapers, organisation in the workplace, street marches, and, if necessary, violent cla-shes and confrontations. The fascists had to be driven off the streets. But this ignored the fact that fascism had made deep inroads into white working-class communities, including many who had fought in the war. The parallel with drug policy was a close one. It was possible to remove the NF and its propaganda from the main streets, but the underlying causes of its popularity remained.

This, of course, raises again the general question which provides an undercurrent for the whole of this book: how can personal care and public witness be held together? A central problem is the fact that the church, and the Church of England in particular, has been much more comfortable with chaplaincy, ambulance and casualty work than it has with

89

any prophetic, critical or political role. It has preferred to comfort the afflicted than to afflict the comfortable, and the ambulance style of ministry is applauded even by those who are themselves largely responsible for the problems it seeks to alleviate. So in 1978 many clergy believed that the appropriate Christian response to the rise of fascism and of racial violence was the quiet 'pastoral' approach of care for victims and influence on the perpetrators, avoiding the political issues where involvement would be divisive and explosive. I was, and remain, deeply unhappy with this approach, and some words of R. H. Tawney from 1912 help to express my unease. Tawney wrote:

> One whole wing of social reformers has gone, it seems to me, altogether astray. They are preoccupied with relieving distress, patching up failures, reclaiming the broken down. All this is good and necessary. But it is not the social problem. . . It is no use giving opiates or stimulants to men whose daily regimen is unhealthy. It is no use devising relief schemes for a community where the normal relationships are felt to be unjust.[2]

In 1978 in Bethnal Green this was precisely our situation.

The East End church context

Behind the preference for personal and casualty caring over social criticism and political action there lay a long history both nationally and locally. In the East End itself there was a long and continuing tradition of Christian philanthropy and care, much of it of Anglican origin. The parish system came relatively late to Bethnal Green. In the Middle Ages the whole of the East End was part of the parish of Stepney. In the early eighteenth century, during the reign of Queen Anne, an Act of Parliament was passed for the building of fifty churches. Only fourteen of them were built, but five of them were in the East End. The parish of Bethnal Green was created in 1742, and St Matthew's church was built several years later. There was no further church building until the 1830s when C. J. Blomfield, the Bishop of London, initiated a decade of church expansion, building ten churches in Bethnal Green in ten years. By the 1870s and 1880s, however, the East End had been virtually colonised by a whole range of movements of rescue, education and care – the settlement movement, ritualism, Wesleyan and evangelical missions, and the Salvation Army, founded in St Matthew's parish in 1865.

Within East End Anglicanism, there were three significant theological and pastoral traditions. First, there was the ritualist movement which established some of its main centres in the area, particularly in London Docks, and in Haggerston and Hoxton. Here there was a stress on dignity and ceremonial in worship, and the movement had splendid and awe-inspiring churches. The early ritualist clergy have an impressive record of personal care, and were actively involved in ministering to victims of the cholera epidemics. They held a strong incarnational theology and their lives were marked by intense personal devotion. But they had, for the most part, no political awareness. The church was seen as a refuge. The theology was pietist, and the clergy were paternalist in their style. The hymns from the ritualist era tell their own story – 'Sweet sacrament divine', 'Sweet heart of Jesus, fount of love and mercy', and many others. Here was the spirituality of the sacred heart, the blessed sacrament, a spirituality of warmth and of comfort rather than of combat or of struggle.

Secondly, there was the evangelical tradition. The East End was for many years something of an evangelical desert, and those churches that did exist tended to be eclectic. Christ Church, Spitalfields, which towered over the market and the streets around Brick Lane, became, in the early 1960s, a centre for work with vagrant alcoholics, and, under the leadership of its parish priest Denis Downham, a lost tradition of social concern and social care was restored. By the late 1970s, and especially during the 1980s, a new breed of radical evangelical was appearing in the area.

Thirdly, there were the 'sacramental socialists',[3] among

whom I would number myself. This was the tradition of Stewart Headlam, John Groser and Stanley Evans.

Often confused with Anglo-Catholicism and ritualism, in fact, the theology of the sacramental socialists was different, and was influenced more by the tradition of F. D. Maurice than by that of Keble and Pusey. It was this tradition which made a close link between the liturgy and social struggle, between prayer and politics, between the Kingdom of God and the social and political struggles of the people.

Combating organised racism

One feature of the sacramental socialists was their use of symbolic and sacramental actions in the streets. During the period of intense NF activity, I recalled John Groser in the 1950s leading a procession with incense, lights and a large pot of red paint, and solemnly painting over one of the early 'Keep Britain White' slogans. In 1978, after two years of NF activity in Bethnal Green Road, Chief Inspector John Wallis said at a public meeting in the Montefiore Centre that they were not breaking any laws. He then, in a comment which he must soon have regretted, suggested that if anti-racists objected to the NF presence, they should arrive on the site first. At this moment I knew what we had to do.

I wrote a letter that evening which was published in the two East End newspapers, calling on all anti-racists to occupy the NF site each Sunday morning from 10 a.m. onwards. Knowing that the NF would turn up at 9 a.m. and the police at 8 a.m., we had secretly arranged to occupy the site from 6 a.m. The occupation began with fifty of us, but within a few weeks it had grown to thousands. It was certainly effective in the short term. It did not break the fascist movement but it did erode its base of mass support and created a counter-force within the area. It brought together Bangladeshis and whites in common cause, and it was a tremendous morale-booster as ordinary people realised their own power and potential when organised and acting together.

Linked with the occupation were two other forms of symbolic action. The first was the removal of racist graffiti from walls and railway bridges. Some of this material had been there for years. Several people were arrested for painting over such graffiti, though to my recollection nobody was ever arrested for putting them there! However, after a court case in which four trade unionists were discharged, the police ceased to make arrests for removals, and many of the most offensive graffiti were washed off or covered up. Again, the action showed that the issue was being taken seriously. Prior to the campaign to remove the graffiti, deeply offensive and threatening slogans and symbols remained for months, a sign to Bangladeshi people and others that the community either did not care or actually agreed with the sentiments expressed. The symbol of the British Movement, a more openly Nazi group than the NF, remained for some months on the wall of Bethnal Green Police Station. Once the removals had started, even the local authority began to wash off slogans.

What aroused the most popular interest, particularly among young people, was a series of rock concerts, linked with the 'Rock Against Racism' movement, culminating in the 80,000 strong 'Carnival Against the Nazis' on 30 April 1978. Rock musicians such as Tom Robinson Band and Steel Pulse led the march through all the strongholds of the fascist presence to a concert in Victoria Park. The effect of the carnival was a very powerful one. Through music and the sheer force of infectious enjoyment, we managed to convey to thousands of people who did not read books or take part in political campaigns that there was a large body of people who really enjoyed, and were committed to, being a multi-racial community. The impact was not at the intellectual level but at that of culture and entertainment. Unlike most demonstrations it opposed racism by fun. By contrast the small band of NF supporters on the sidewalk looked extremely miserable and dull. The slogan 'NF = No Fun', which was associated with the carnivals, was extremely effective.

However, more important and much more difficult was the work of undermining the appeal of the NF and the provision of alternatives. As with drug work, without more hopeful alternatives, relapse is inevitable. This long term work was, and is, much more demanding, and many who were happy to join in demos and protests were not ready for the slow, boring activity which was needed. Racism and fascism feed on deep social discontents and transform them into prejudice and violence. Only by undermining the basis for their appeal, by attending to the conditions and needs which made the fascist analysis plausible, could the damage be reduced and the forward march of the NF be halted. We had to show that we cared more about the elderly and the alienated youth, about bad housing, and about areas of neglect than the fascists did. We had to recognise that most people who were drawn to the NF were not hard core fascists but decent people who felt betrayed and ignored by the other parties and institutions. The rise of the NF was a challenge to other movements, including churches, to get our act together, and to renew our own commitment to justice and the defence of minorities. That struggle goes on. In the East End the power of the NF was broken by a combination of internal conflicts, and external political developments within the mainstream parties, in particular by the swing to the Conservatives in 1979.

Racism: its changing character

In January 1978, as the tension was mounting in Bethnal Green and racial attacks were increasing nationally, Margaret Thatcher was interviewed on Granada TV's World in Action programme. What is now remembered about this interview is her expression of the view that people were 'rather afraid' that the British character, culture and way of life were in danger of being 'swamped' by an influx of alien people. However, in that interview she was also asked about the success of the National Front. Gordon Burns, the interviewer, said, 'So some of the support that the National Front has been attracting in recent by-elections you would hope to bring back

94

behind the Tory Party?' Mrs Thatcher replied, 'Oh very much back, certainly. . .'⁴ This was in fact what happened. Within days of Mrs Thatcher's interview the Conservatives had jumped ahead of Labour in the polls. At the General Election in 1979, in every area in Greater London where the NF had shown signs of success, from Islington Central through the East End to Dagenham, there was a major swing to the Conservatives. There is no doubt that opposition to black immigration, and the belief that the Conservatives were now committed to a 'hard line' on immigration, was a major factor in their success in the election. The fascist parties had in a sense become obsolete as the expression of racist sentiments became increasingly acceptable within the Conservative Party.

What we have seen during the Thatcher years has been the gentrification of racism. While the NF and its satellites have continued to mobilise, in spite of serious splits and setbacks, and in some areas still form a serious physical threat to minority communities, what has been most marked has been the integration of racial nationalism into the mainstream of party politics. This is, of course, not peculiar to the Conservative Party nor is it entirely new. Certainly it is during the Thatcher period that the articulation of crude racism seems to have become more acceptable than in previous years. But we are witnessing the culmination of a process which was begun with the agitation against the West Indian presence in the 1950s, and with the movement for immigration control based on colour discrimination. Behind this highly successful movement, and the legislation since 1962 which has resulted from it, have been two assumptions.

First, the assumption that black people are intrinsically problematic, by the very fact of their existence. They are responsible for increased racism. (In similar vein Sir Oswald Mosley had said that the Jews were the cause of anti-semitism.) If they were not present, there would be no racism. The more of them there are in an area, the more racial prejudice, discrimination, tension and violence there will be. Ruth Glass once called this colour calculus view 'a new doctrine of original sin combined with a new faulty political arithmetic'.[5] At one time politicians of left and right were somewhat embarrassed by the colour basis of the demand for control and used to throw in the odd reference to the fact that controls would be 'irrespective of race, colour or creed' (though few were convinced by such assurances). Today, however, the openly racial basis of the legislation is widely accepted.

The second assumption – which would, of course, be meaningless without the acceptance of the first – is that racial discrimination at the doors of Britain is somehow necessary in order to produce racial harmony within Britain. Tight immigration control, it is claimed, promotes racial harmony. Not only is this illogical, since it seeks to use racial discrimination in one place as a means of reducing it in another, but it is contradicted by the historical evidence. It is in fact during the years in which immigration controls have been in operation that there has been a hardening of attitudes and a deterioration in the racial climate. Each set of controls generates further demands for tighter controls. The obsession with control, and the amount of money and energy spent on implementing such control, stands in stark contrast with the lack of commitment and resources which have been put into combating discrimination. It is not a recipe for harmony, let alone justice. Nevertheless the thesis continues to be repeated ritually by politicians of both major parties as if everyone knew it was true.

Since the 1960s these assumptions have been incorporated into legislation and have been the basis of government policies on race. The Labour Party opposed the 1962 Commonwealth Immigrants Act (described in its preamble as a temporary provision) as a measure based on colour prejudice, but when in power they both renewed and strengthened it. The White Paper of 1965 has rightly been described as the foundation document of modern racism.[6] Further legislation is 1968 and 1971 strengthened the racial basis of control. The devaluing of the British passport in the 'Kenyan Asians' legislation of 1968 prefigured the problems which we are currently seeing in relation to Hong Kong. Finally the British Nationality Act of 1981 set the seal on the racial understanding of nationality and citizenship. By the time of the 1987 General Election race relations and immigration control were virtually identified in the Conservative Party's promotional literature.[7] Increasingly the idea has been established that to be truly British is to be white. The white inhabitants of mainland Britain, the Northern Irish and the Falkland Islanders are seen as more authentically British than black people who were born here. Indeed, had the Falkland Islanders been black, the war would not have been fought at all.

So today we have what Martin Barker has termed a 'new racism'[8] though it is questionable, even on his own evidence, how new it is. What he and other writers mean is that today's racism is no longer rooted, or at least no longer stated, in terms of an explicit doctrine of superiority, genetic or otherwise, but in a particular understanding of culture and national identity. It is a genteel racism, though its manifestations in the back streets may be far from genteel. It coexists with race relations legislation, equal opportunities policies, and a range of initiatives which do not significantly disturb the structures of inequality. Black people are accepted so long as they toe the line and know their place. But essentially they are an alien wedge. When our leaders speak of 'our people' or 'the British character', black people are not normally included. When Mrs Thatcher, in her Cheltenham 'victory speech' after the Falklands war, said that Britain was a nation which once ruled an empire, she conveniently forgot that black people did not rule an empire: they were ruled by it.

It is here that the real significance of that enigmatic figure Enoch Powell lies. For as Peregrine Worsthorne has pointed out, what we now call Thatcherism was once called Powellism.[9] Although Powell himself has become something of a wilderness figure, many of his concerns and demands have been incorporated into mainstream government thinking, discourse and policy. With the increasing shift of the daily press to the extreme right, and, in the case of papers such as *The Sun*, *The Star* and the *Daily Mail*, to the racist right, we now find that organisations such as the NF are doubly obsolete. Obsolete at the level of theory because so many of their demands are now part of state policy and legislation, obsolete at the level of polemic because the crude racist rhetoric which was once their distinctive contribution to British political life has now become more acceptable within the tabloid news-papers.[10]

Racism and the church

How has the church responded to the issues of race and racism? In all honesty, not very well. For many years, it did not respond at all. Racism – or rather 'the colour problem', for that was the language of those early years of the 50s and 60s, occurred somewhere else. There had been a major study by Joe Oldham in 1924, and William Temple, later Arch-bishop of Canterbury, had reviewed it, commenting that race was the most important issue facing the church.[11] But this was a freak incident, and neither Oldham's concern nor Temple's support for it was reflected in church thinking or policy in Britain for many years. Few Christians in Britain made con-nections between developments in South Africa or the United States and those in British cities and towns. At the official level race was ignored by theologians and policy makers. As late as 1974 the Advisory Council for the Church's Ministry (ACCM) produced a textbook for teaching Christian ethics in Anglican theological colleges. The final draft, while it included several pages on issues of sexual ethics, dealt with the whole question of race in eight lines, including a rec-ommendation of Anthony Richmond's book *The Colour Prob-lem*, published in the 1950s. After protests by the present author, some small improvements were made, mainly in the bibliography. No attention was paid to racism as such or to the issues raised by black theology.[12] One might have hoped that ACCM would have learned something over the next decade, but sadly this was not the case. John Tiller's study of the future of the Anglican ministry, published in 1983, virtually ignored the existence of black people in the Church of England.[13]

The neglect was not peculiar to Anglicans. In 1980 a study was made of ten theological colleges on the extent to which students were being prepared for work in a multi-racial and multi-faith society. In his preface, Professor John Hick claimed that unless there were major changes, the next generation of clergy were likely to be 'blind leaders of the blind' in this area.[14] In 1984 a study of attitudes to race and racism in the Roman Catholic Church reported that 'in none of the seminaries did we find a clear and explicit commitment to preparing future priests to exercise their ministry in a racially mixed and culturally diverse society'. Indeed the report concluded that 'the development of an awareness of institutional and personal racism does not appear to be part of the seminarians' training'.[15] Heather Walton's study of Methodism in 1985 noted a similar lack of preparation in Methodist theological colleges,[16] while one submission to the Archbishop's Commission on Urban Priority Areas claimed that theological training had 'positively unfitted [clergy] for an inner urban ministry'.[17]

Of course, it would be grossly unfair to leave it at this point. There has been much concern, and much action rooted in concern, about race relations and the conditions of black people at the localised level. But the tendency until recently has been to see race relations as an aspect of personal relations. With good will and kindness, harmony could be created without any serious conflict. The emphasis has mainly been on racial harmony rather than on racial justice, and the issues have been seen in essentially personal terms. Racial prejudice has been seen purely in terms of personal sin, to be dealt with at the personal level. Linked with this moral and individual approach has been an emphasis on education. If racial prejudice is due to sin, it is also related to ignorance. If it cannot be removed, it can at least be reduced, by the dissemination of facts, by raising the level of awareness. Churches have shared in the belief which has been general in liberal society in the value of facts to overcome irrational and ignorant positions.

In recent years particularly, there has been a good deal of support for projects in multi-racial areas, though this has been very uneven as the history of the Race Relations Projects Fund of the British Council of Churches has shown. Although the General Synod of the Church of England in 1979 called on all dioceses to give support, to this day there has been virtually no support or interest shown by such dioceses as Exeter, Blackburn, Truro, Carlisle, Durham and Peterborough – or, indeed, by Bradford, in spite of considerable activity by church groups within the city itself.

The churches' response to race issues has been marked by a number of weaknesses. There has been little comprehension of white racism. Rather has racism been seen as a problem associated exclusively with the presence of black people in certain areas. 'We don't have the problem here' is still one of the most widely heard comments in those dioceses where the Church of England is statistically most effective. But to say that there are no problems of racism because there are no, or few, black people is rather like saying that there are no problems of sex in a boys' school because of the absence of girls. In fact racism is deeply embedded in areas which are predominantly white. Most of the really vicious racist and anti-semitic literature, including the notorious 'holocaust denial' propaganda, emanates from the diocese of Chichester in Sussex.

There has been very little understanding of the structural nature of racism. It was in fact precisely to assert this structural dimension that the word 'racism' came into common usage at the end of the 1960s. (It does not appear in most dictionaries prior to this period.) But most Christians in the west have not understood structural evil, nor have they been helped by their teachers to do so. They have not seen that racism, like social inequality, injustice, gender disadvantage, and so on are rooted in structural patterns which can only be changed at the structural level. It was because Leonardo Boff raised the issues of power in the church that he got into difficulties with the Vatican: had he remained at the level of ideas he would probably have been safe. Boff's words are of vital importance in understanding systemic racism.

> Unfortunately conversion is interpreted in such a way that allows the power structure to remain as it is. An intimate and private meaning is given to conversion. . . Institutions have a life of their own, independent of the good or ill intentions of individuals within them. If conversion does not reach the institution of the church, if it does not call into question the way in which power is exercised, if it does not reach the wider society, then we cannot speak of gospel conversion. We end up with extremely good-willed individuals with pure intentions but who are faithful, loyal and uncritical toward the institution, who through this institution cause serious damage to people and to the church. Pascal noted that evil is not so powerfully achieved as when it is done with good will and purity of heart.[18]

So it is striking that no diocese in the Church of England has even begun to take positive action policies to combat racial inequality. Church House, the national headquarters of the Church of England, which on most matters follows the Civil Service more faithfully than the gospel, has still failed to follow them in the two areas of ethnic monitoring and equal opportunities. The Commission for Racial Equality's Code of Practice on employment policy, which has 'increasingly become standard personnel practice'[19] is still largely unknown throughout the churches. When asked why this was so, the personnel officer at Church House commented that 'everyone knows that the church doesn't discriminate'.

There has been a resistance too, to making connections. In this the churches have merely followed secular bureaucratic fashion, as they have done in most areas. Race relations, like many other issues, has become compartmentalised. But there has been a facet of this compartmentalising which is peculiar to the church, and it relates to its most fundamental weakness in tackling racism.

For, most serious of all, there has been a failure to think evangelically about racism, to relate it to the nature of the

101

gospel, the understanding of God and the world. During six years as an employee of Church House, I found that people got very embarrassed when one tried to bring God and theology into discussions about policy. There was lip service to 'biblical principles' but they usually only related to sex and personal morality, not to investments, interest on loans, equal opportunities policies, or indeed any policies.

How has the church responded to racism? I have not answered the question, for I have only responded to it in terms of the 'mainstream' white-led churches. I have in fact answered it in a racist way as if the entire church in Britain were white-led. In fact, the fastest growing Christian churches are black-led, churches such as the New Testament Church of God, the Church of God of Prophecy, and many others, mainly Pentecostal in theology. It is essential to realise that the growth of the black-led churches is a post-immigration phenomenon. At the time of the beginning of immigration from the Caribbean, around 90 per cent of practising Christians in the islands belonged to 'mainstream' churches – Anglican, Roman Catholic, Baptist, Methodist and Moravian – and less than 10 per cent to the so-called 'sideways' churches, mainly Pentecostal groups based in Jamaica. Today in Britain almost the reverse is the case.

Well over 70 per cent of Christians of Afro-Caribbean origin belong to independent black-led churches, and the numbers are increasing. Even if one ignores this enormous area of black Christianity, it is also true that in many inner-city areas the bulk of practising Christians in the 'mainstream' churches are black (though the power is still in white hands). The future of organised Christianity in many British cities may well lie in the hands of black Christians.

Theology and racial justice

I cannot here outline an agenda for the churches on racial justice but I will conclude this chapter with some general comments, based on my own experience.

First, it is important to see that racism presents a fundamental, not an accidental, challenge to the nature of the gospel and the church. Catholicity, wholeness, universality, is an essential defining characteristic of the people of God. From the Epistles to the Ephesians and Colossians onwards, Christian teaching about salvation has held that, through the cross, the divisions in the human family have been abolished. There is a new unified humanity (Eph. 2:15). The church is seen as a new race (1 Peter 2:9), a community born not of blood nor of the will of the flesh but of God (John 1:13), a community in whom the divine seed dwells (1 John 3:9). The overcoming of the wall of division between Jews and Gentiles and the creation of a new humanity is central to the New Testament understanding of Christianity. That understanding has to be manifested in real terms. It is undermined and contradicted by racism, tribalism and ethnocentricity. It is equally undermined by the kind of religion which acts merely as a reinforcement of the old order, reinforcing racism in the process.

Secondly, we need to see that racism is about power relations and interests, not simply about ideas. The church is much happier at the level of ideas as long as they do not lead to conflicts with its interests. Karl Marx wrote that the Church of England would sooner abandon thirty-eight of its thirty-nine articles than one thirty-ninth of its income.[20] But the struggle against racism will make no real progress if it stays at the level of ideas, and the church, like most institutions, fears any threat to its interests.

Thirdly, it is necessary to recognise both the specificity and the concreteness of racism, and also its connectedness with other levels of disadvantage and oppression. This involves the recognition that racial oppression cannot be 'dissolved' into issues of class or gender or 'common humanity' or anything else. This is both a denial of reality and a recipe for inaction. But it also involves a realisation that connections and alliances can only be made in the course of struggle. Alliances must be alliances of the committed, not the pseudo-connections made by those whose aim is to prevent change.

I am suggesting in fact that racism is a litmus test or a barium meal by which a whole range of evils and injustices and levels of oppression in society will be exposed, and this points to the fact that there are two different views of the nature of racism which underlie many of the conflicts about anti-racist strategy. There is a 'coat of paint' view in which racial discrimination and disadvantage are seen as pathological growths upon a basically healthy society. They are diseases of the body politic. They are not endemic. They can be dealt with – by education, by consciousness raising, by therapy (Racism Awareness Training) – without any fundamental disturbance to the fabric of society.

The second view – which I hold – is that racism manifests in specific and visible ways more fundamental injustices and contradictions within the social structure. Thus to disturb the racial balance is to disturb the whole system. Those who become involved in the struggle for racial justice should expect that struggle to lead them on to take seriously other related issues.

My experience has been that, whether we are dealing with homelessness, drug use or the problems of racial minorities, concern about social justice does not normally arise from a vague sense of the need to correct generalised oppression. It arises from very specific and localised struggles which then lead us to make connections with wider issues.

5

What's in it for Whitechapel Road?

Ministry, Liberation and the City

Caring and justice

As I reflect on twenty-five years as a priest in inner London,
I look back upon a church which has, for the most part, been
prepared to accept its role as one of caring for the wounded,
ministering to the needs of the victims, but has been reluctant
to take on the role of interfering with the structures of power.
The words of Amaziah, the priest of Bethel, addressed to the
prophet Amos, constantly come back to me.

> O seer, go, flee away to the land of Judah, and eat bread
> there, and prophesy there; but never again prophesy at
> Bethel, for it is the king's sanctuary, and it is a temple of
> the kingdom (Amos 7:12–13).

So, as I examine my ministry and that of my colleagues, I
find a recurring pattern. We have dealt with abscesses, coped
with overdoses, and contacted addicts' families. We have
provided beds and food for the homeless. We have supported
the victims of racial violence. All this has been acceptable.
What has not been acceptable has been concern about, and
action against, the root causes of drug abuse, homelessness,
and racism, concern and action which is bound to have an
effect within the economic and political arena, and yet I have
found over and over again that, through our personal caring,
we have been led to act on the wider issues of justice.

Thus in caring for the teenage amphetamine user, we were
held to ask questions about the ethics of manufacturers'

105

claims, about the therapeutic justification for the manufacture
of certain products, about the conflict between the 'research'
cited by marketing divisions of certain companies and the
results of independent clinical research, and about doctors'
prescribing methods. In caring for heroin addicts, we were
led to question a 'system' which offered control without care,
which was concerned to prohibit and to wage war more than
it was to learn from the lessons of past history that such
methods were doomed not only to fail but to aggravate the
problem. We found ourselves over and over again confronted
by bureaucratic lying, by claims which did not correspond to
the reality which we saw. In working with young drug takers,
we were led to oppose the hysterical and ill-informed accounts
in the mass media which led many young people to lose all
confidence in drug information emanating from adult sources.
And we were led to look at the economic origins of the
international drug traffic, at conditions in the Third World,
and to realise that without alternative economies there would
be no end to the heroin and cocaine trade.

Similarly, in our work with the young homeless, it became
clear within a month of forming Centrepoint that the contribution of Glasgow to the problem of single homelessness in
London was well in excess of its size, and that no amount of
attention at the point of arrival would have any effect if the
problems at source were not tackled. We were not able to
ignore the immense problems of economic poverty and the
role of government policies in creating a new 'underclass'.
We have seen homelessness become dramatically more serious
during the last decade. We have seen the increase in the
numbers of beggars, in the expansion of the world of the
young prostitutes, including a large number whose motive is
sheer economic survival – 'Thatcher's girls' was the name
given to them in the Kings Cross district several years ago.
We have noticed the increase in the number of teeange sui-
cides and of young people who have become mentally ill as
a result of homelessness. We have witnessed the decline in
cheap rented accommodation in London, while whole areas

are gentrified and yuppified, and churches are subdivided into luxury flats for the very wealthy.

All these facts are well-known and well-documented, and the experience of pastoral work has driven home their urgency. Yet to listen to government spokespersons, including cabinet ministers, is to enter a world of absurdity, of culpable ignorance, of untruth. In fact the higher one rises in the political hierarchy the greater seems to be the degree of ignorance of social reality. It is no longer a simple comprehension gap: it is a conflict in the whole understanding of the nature of truth. Sadly, even good men and women seem not to notice the more glaring facts about homelessness. Recently four of the more intelligent of our public figures – Fay Weldon, Michael Heseltine, Enoch Powell and Tony Benn – when asked a question on the causes of homelessness on the Radio 4 programme Any Questions (23 December 1989) focussed on the discharge of patients from psychiatric hospitals as if this were the major cause, ignoring the far more significant factors of the decline in the private rented sector and of migration from the deprived areas of the north.

My own pastoral experience, however, has not simply been that of making connections from personal to political: it has been a painful saga of seeing one's own values and commitments violated, and one's own work consistently undermined and damaged, by political decisions and policies. Of course, one carries on. The work of picking up the pieces of racism has continued in spite of the persistent hostility towards immigrants, the ever increasing tendency as we move towards 1992 to link illegal immigrants with drugs and terrorism, the use of the police as agents of racist laws, the exploitation of prejudice and ignorance by leading political figures combined with the lack of any lead from the centre in combating racism. But it has all been a case of swimming against the tide.

In all these areas compassion has replaced justice. An unjust society makes provision within it for the exercise of care and compassion, but care and compassion conflict with injustice and institutionalised cruelty, and we have lost any sense of the meaning of justice. For justice can only exist

107

within a framework which recognises the existence of society and of responsibilities within society. Our culture, however, has become increasingly dominated by the anti-Christian and anti-social notion of privatisation.

Private care and public testimony

In our society the split between private and public realms has become endemic. Religion clearly belongs in the realm of the private. Not in the sense that it is seen to have no public function, but that its public function is that of the moral and spiritual reinforcement and nourishment of the private individuals who constitute the public realm. So words which arose within a public context and held a public reference – liturgy, counselling, religion itself – now acquire a private and subcultural meaning which does not directly connect with the public realm, and this political and cultural context has its theological equivalent. For theological individualism has been a governing principle of most of western Christianity since the Reformation. Theological individualism grew up as the religious equivalent of laissez-faire economics. The corporate religious framework of feudalism gave way to a framework where the fate of the individual soul became central. Theological individualism is more highly developed in the United States than in Britain, and it was out of this tradition that the pastoral counselling movement developed. So as managers became the symbols of the public realm, so did therapists and counsellors become the guardians of the realm of the private.

The public sector, including the church bureaucracies, is controlled by civil servants and managers, people who combine manipulative expertise with a supposed value-neutrality. The social machinery is seen as objective, scientific, government by experts, and increasingly is not subject to question. Dysfunction within this society is seen as personal dysfunction; and so the counsellor, the social worker and the various therapeutic disciplines are brought in to enable the personal dysfunction to be healed.

In our society, the counsellor, the social worker, and the therapist play increasingly important roles. In political terms, they can be seen as the scavengers of the capitalist system. They pick up the pieces, care for the casualties, and sometimes restore broken people to the public realm. They represent in secularised form what has already happened to Christian pastoral ministry.

The phrase 'scavengers of the capitalist system' was first used by Canon Percy Widdrington in 1913, and his words are as applicable now as when he first used them – perhaps more so. Addressing a conference of the Church Socialist League at Coventry, he said:

> The church has been too long the Church Quiescent here on earth, content to serve as the scavenger of the capitalist system. If it refuses the challenge it may survive as a pietistic sect providing devotional opportunities for a small and dwindling section of the community, a residuary solace for the world's defeated, administering religion as an anaesthetic to help men to endure the hateful operation of life, an ambulance picking up the wounded, entered on the Charities Register – an institution among institutions. But it will cease to be the organ of the Kingdom, building up the world out of itself: it will have abandoned its mission and become apostate.[1]

My experience has been that it is because of its role as scavenger, gap-filler, picking up the pieces, that the church is valued in our society, and that in the present climate there is a real danger that many sections of the church will accept this role. To do so would be a disastrous theological and political mistake.

There is, however, another aspect of the church's ministry which is highly valued by politicians: that of moral leadership. Douglas Hurd's address to the General Synod in February 1988 stated this approach clearly[2] The Church's territory lies firmly within the realm of the maintenance and restoration of moral and spiritual values. However, 'moral' tends to be restricted to the areas of sexuality, the family, and law and order, 'spiritual' to those of the inner world and life after death. Major issues such as peace, justice, the defence of the poor and oppressed, are labelled 'political'. Neither the area of ambulance work nor that of moral preservation involves any questioning of the status quo or any critique of the dominant value system. Indeed to move into the area of questioning and critique is seen as a deviation from authentic spirituality and from 'tradition'. Those who oppose such actions are often described nowadays as 'traditionalists'.

Just how modern and untraditional is such a viewpoint is brought out in some words written by Maurice Reckitt in 1935.

> If you had told any typical Christian thinker in any century from the twelfth to the sixteenth that religion had nothing to do with economics, and that bishops must not intrude in these matters upon the deliberations of laymen – propositions which to many of the correspondents to our newspapers appear to be axiomatic – he would either have trembled for your faith or feared for your reason. He would have regarded you, in short, as either a heretic or a lunatic.[3]

The notion of salvation and of the work of the church as being primarily or even exclusively personal and inward is a characteristically modern one.

The notion has been particularly damaging in the field of pastoral care. A very limited understanding of the pastoral task has come to be accepted by the church as well as by secular groups. Thus Peter Selby can write that 'the heightening of dissatisfaction, the arousing of a deep longing for the rectification of the social causes of distress – these do not appear very often, in print or in our heads, as goals of the pastoral enterprise'.[4] Pastoral care has come to be seen as politically neutral. Indeed to take sides, to espouse positions on public issues, is seen as undermining pastoral work. A fascinating illustration of this view of pastoral care occurred in a job description for the rectorship of a parish in East

110

Anglia in which there was a nuclear power station. After listing the qualities sought in the new incumbent, the document ended with the words: 'It is most important that the new rector is not an anti-nuclear campaigner since this would divide the parish and make pastoral work impossible.' The assumptions contained here were very revealing: that one position would divide while another would not; that 'divisiveness' was to be associated with having strong principles rather than weak ones; that divisiveness and pastoral work did not go well together; and that if somehow the parish could find a rector who had no views whatsoever on such an important subject, that would be the most 'pastoral' way forward.

In my experience, and in the fields of ministry with which I have been concerned in this book particularly, one of the most damaging features of recent church life has been the reduction of pastoral ministry to a counselling model. The counsellor who is concerned with problem solving and derives his or her skills mainly from clinical and psychotherapeutic sources comes to be the model of Christian pastoral care. But this represents a grave distortion of what pastoral care is about. It can only be adequately conceived and practised if we can hold together personal and political dimensions, and specifically three areas: the defence of the oppressed, the conflict with principalities and powers, and the proclamation of, and witness to, the truth. To reduce pastoral ministry to counselling is a distortion which fits very comfortably within the individualist framework of thought but takes no account of the social theology of the scriptures where the emphasis is on the people of God, the Kingdom, the Body of Christ, the new creation.

Pastoral care in the Christian tradition is a ministry of the whole community. Overemphasis on professionalism, on skills and techniques, and on casework will obscure the nature of a caring and supportive community. It is a particularly serious misrepresentation of the Christian pastoral ministry to identify it with problem solving. In the classic tradition the work of counsel and guidance is known as spiritual direction. Its central focus is union with God and discernment of the will of God for one's life. It is not problem-centred but God-centred. Its context is not the office or the clinic but the Christian community. The identification of pastoral care with 'ministry to deeply troubled persons' produces what Robert Lambourne called a 'hang-up theology' in which human progress is perceived in terms of clinical models of problem identification and resolution.[5]

We will only recover our bearings when we recognise the unity of personal and political, of pastoral and prophetic ministry. Indeed one of the central elements in our confusion is a profound misunderstanding of the role of the shepherd. The way in which the term 'shepherding' has been used in the clinical theological literature from Seward Hiltner to Frank Lake bears no relationship to its origin or its practice and must be one of the most astonishing examples of linguistic gymnastics in recent history.[6] The idea of a shepherd has nothing to do with clinical pastoral models. It is a ministry of public care, defence and leadership, as in Ezekiel 34, and to bring Ezekiel into the discussion is to raise the question of the relationship between pastoral care and prophecy.

Can pastors be prophets?

The conventional wisdom contrasts pastors and prophets. They are seen as representing distinct, conflicting styles of ministry, possibly determined by temperament. Certainly it is assumed that prophets make bad pastors, and that pastors cannot be prophetic without jeopardising their essential work. But to oppose pastoral and prophetic traditions in this way is questionable. For without the prophetic consciousness and the prophetic vision, pastoral care is likely, maybe certain, to degenerate into ambulance work, a style of ministry full of care and concern, devoid of vision and challenge, a pastoral project without theology.

Prophecy is an assault on the public imagination, a raiding of lost traditions, a seizing upon an alternative consciousness. Walter Brueggeman rightly sees the prophet as a destabilising presence within society.[7] This is because the prophetic consciousness represents the principle of surprise, of newness, of subversive memory, of protest rooted in a tradition which has been forgotten. Without the prophetic spirit, religion inevitably becomes complacent, weary, obsessed with security and comfort, captive to the tyranny of the age. Prophecy is an attack on weariness (Jeremiah 9:5). It is the role of the prophet to ask impossible questions, to challenge the conventions, to arouse those who have gone to sleep. At the heart of the prophetic consciousness is the struggle for a new vision. The prophet is more concerned to see clearly than to behave well. In most societies prophetic figures are maladjusted, not adjusted. They belong with those whom Luther King called the creatively maladjusted.

But a church which is run by managers, administered by bureaucrats, and assisted by therapists and counsellors will find prophetic maladjustment hard to cope with. It will tend to work with the dominant system, seeking to ameliorate and reform, to enable the system to function in a more human and compassionate way, but all within the framework of structures which are accepted. This is the theology of *Faith in the City* and *Changing Britain*. As the former says:

> Christians can hardly be expected to propose a realistic alternative to the entire economic system, but there is ample precedent in the Christian tradition for exposing the system we have to critical scrutiny.[8]

So at a time when many people are proposing realistic alternatives, it seems that Christians, who claim some access to the grace of God, are inferior to, or less well equipped than, others within the human family at this stage in our economic and political history. Theologically the statement is highly suspect. For there is a persistent strain in Christian history which claims that the gospel is actually about an alternative vision, an alternative lifestyle, an alternative kingdom, an alternative world. Rather than providing props and bandages, counsellors and therapists, reforms and revisions, ought not

113

the church to be exhibiting an alternative community, a zone of truth and justice? Stanley Hauerwas has suggested that

> the church's great failure in social ethics has not merely been her willingness to support the status quo but her inability to stand as an alternative to the current forms of the political.[9]

Prophetic ministry is about alternatives. The prophet addresses the specific conditions, and within that context demands change. If this is not an integral part of the pastoral ministry, it is difficult to know what is.

The need for a street theology

Yet while there is a prophetic dimension in pastoral care, there is a crucial difference between the prophet and most other forms of religious life. The prophet arises within, and speaks to, a situation of crisis. Prophetic ministry, unlike that of the scholar, the pastor, the theologian, the scribe, or the moralist, occurs within a concrete and highly specific situation, a situation calling for urgency, and for extreme and dramatic intervention. Yet prophecy cannot exist apart from the other forms, apart from the ongoing life of a religious community. Without that life and its assumptions, prophecy makes no sense and cannot be heard. For a prophetic ministry to appear in the back streets there needs to be a street theological tradition out of which it arises and which can respond to it. This does not, of course, mean that prophetic figures will not, and do not, arise within the deformed wastes of our culture, and they will make connections with elements within our history and memory. They will, in the main, be voices of protest, negative voices, crying against the dominant system. They will be wilderness voices, and only rarely will movements of prophetic creativity arise to nurture them and to develop their vision.

My experience of ministry in the back streets has made me more aware of the need for good theology, for theology which

114

is integrated with the struggles of specific communities, for a street theology. But to say this is to raise the problem of the present captivity of theology, the urgent need for the liberation of theology, and for a liberation theology for Britain. Since my student days I have felt a sense of frustration, leading at times to anger and confusion, about the gulf between academic and pastoral activity, about the professionalisation of theology and of pastoral care, and about the whole culture of 'churchianity' which encourages these things to continue.

My main experience of academic theology was at Oxford in the early 1960s where it was possible to graduate and to know nothing about events or thinking beyond the fourth century, and at the University of Chicago in the 1970s and 80s where there was an acute sense of the disconnectedness of the academy from the life of the streets around it. In Britain in particular, theology has come to be seen as something done *by* members of a caste (white, middle-class, male and clerical) *for* 'the people' (who, on the whole, do not want it, and do not see its relevance). The closer one gets to this academic theological world, the further one gets from the life and culture of the back streets.

Of course the captivity of theology is only one part of a much wider problem affecting serious thought within western society. As MacIntyre has commented, 'the attempted professionalisation of serious and systematic thinking has had a disastrous effect upon our culture'.[10] Happily theology, the work of wrestling with God and with the issues around belief in God's actions in the world, does not cease to exist among people simply because it has come to be seen as a job for professionals. It is the professionals who are badly damaged. But theology is damaged also. In Dorothee Soelle's words:

What is called scientific theology is normally conveyed in a language devoid of a sense of awareness. It is unaware of the emotions, insensitive to what people experience. It has no interest and no appeal: it has a dull flatness because it leaves no room for doubt, that shadow of the faith. . .

115

Any theology that wants to communicate with real people must however use a language that shows awareness, brings them and their problems into the dialogue, and is forceful. This grows from practical experience and leads to a change in being and behaviour.[11]

Soelle here points to three problems in academic theology: the neglect of the emotions, feelings and experience; the absence of doubt; and the loss of dialogue. She adds that such a situation can only change as a result of practical experience.

There seems to me to be a three-fold captivity of theology in the west. There is an academic captivity – to do with where theology is done; a cultural captivity – to do with who does theology; and a political captivity – to do with the context in which theology is done, and in whose interests. First of all, theology has been ghettoised within the rarified world of university and seminary. Within this context, it has been distorted into a preparation for ministry, a preparation for doing some other job better. The process by which this occurred, especially since the seventeenth and eighteenth centuries, has been described by Edward Farley.[12] Farley shows that, as a result of the Enlightenment, theology ceased to be seen as a *habitus*, a way of life, and became a systematic body of knowledge and skills. We see this process most highly developed in the Divinity Schools of American universities, such as the University of Chicago, and it is from there that the beginnings of a protest against it can be heard. Thus David Tracy in his 'social portrait of the theologian' defends the public role of the theologian as one who must speak beyond the academy.[13] There have been earlier protests against the reduction of theology to an academic discipline, unconnected with spiritual life, pastoral care and social struggle. The Eastern Orthodox tradition never accepted it, and for many years the Anglican pastoral tradition in England, with its emphasis on learned parish clergy, was a limited attempt to prevent the academic captivity of theological work, at least as far as the clergy were concerned. Yet that captivity has occurred all over the western world. Recently the content

116

WHAT'S IN IT FOR WHITECHAPEL ROAD?

and method of the white male theological establishment has
been subjected to a major critique from those influenced by
liberation theology, including black and feminist theologians.
Yet many, perhaps most, of these critics themselves still operate from within the academic ghetto, and there seems little
concern to undermine that rarified world which continues to
cut off theology from the common people, and to prevent
access to theological work by those who have not been
initiated into its esoteric language and skills.

Linked with the academic captivity is a cultural captivity.
For the world of the theologian is a world cut off from that
of ordinary people, indeed protected against them. One of the
ways in which this separation has been preserved is through
the association of theology with classical culture. Indeed, from
the point of view of this tradition, classical culture is culture.
Bernard Lonergan wrote about this in 1972:

> On classicist assumptions there is just one culture. That
> one culture is not attained by the simple faithful, the people,
> the natives, the barbarians. None the less, career is always
> open to talent. One enters upon such a career by diligent
> study of the ancient Latin or Greek authors. One pursues
> such a career by learning scholastic philosophy and the-
> ology. One aims at high office by becoming proficient in
> canon law. One succeeds by winning the approbation and
> favour of the right personages. Within this set-up the unity
> of faith is a matter of everyone subscribing to the correct
> formulae.[14]

There are three features of this classical tradition. The culture
of the classics is only necessary for the elite, the professionals,
the clergy. The simple faithful don't need it. Theology is a
tradition which is handed down by a caste for the masses.
Diversity ('local theologies', plurality of cultures, and so on)
is a threat to the system.

Theology is thus something done at the top, filtered down,
if at all, very slowly and selectively. Hence all the fuss about
such writers as John Robinson, David Jenkins and Leonardo
Boff. This is why *The Last Temptation of Christ* should not be

117

seen. You can't trust the simple faithful with exposure to questioning. They need to be protected from it. So arises the need for soundness, for the correct line, possibly for infallibility, for what Austin Farrer once called 'an infallible fact factory going full blast'.

The professionalisation of theology has, of course, undergone a major transformation, especially within liberal Protestant and Anglican traditions. The clergy are still seen as technicians, paid carers, professionals, but now they acquire different skills.

> So clergy learn less Greek, Latin, Hebrew and classical theology, but more social science. They become a series of semi-professional therapists with a roving brief, generic case workers for the parish with a mildly spiritual aura.[15]

But there is another facet of the cultural captivity of theology which has become glaringly clear in the last decade. It is not just to do with the content and the concept of skills, but with who the practitioners are, and they are, for the most part, white, middle-class, male clerics. So theology takes on a racist complexion as, within a multi-racial society, and within a Christian community in which black people are a significant presence, theological education 'suffers from its enclosure within an exclusively European, not to say Anglo-Saxon, cultural framework'.[16]

Then there is a political captivity. There is in British political life a long-standing mistrust of dogma and of theory, a devotion to pragmatic and piecemeal reform. It was from politics, not religion, that the use of the word 'theology' as a synonym for irrelevant, archaic theorising originated. But today we are witnessing a recovery of dogma in political life – dogmas such as the free market, free choice, and so on – combined with a rejection of too much dogma in religious life. Churches are supported and valued to the extent that they provide spiritual and moral reinforcement for the political order, but not for their theological scrutiny or vision, for a theologically aware church will be a critical church.

We need to understand where we are before we can move.

If theology is in need of liberation, in need of being reclaimed as 'an essential component of every Christian's kit bag',[17] what needs to be done? How can theology be practised by grass-roots Christian communities? I suggest that we need to hold together four polarities: that theology is both ordinary and extraordinary; that it is both corporate and solitary; that it is both critical and traditional; and that, while it cannot be done by theologians, it cannot be done without them.

First, theology is part of the ordinary activity of the people of God. 'A theologian is one whose prayer is true.'[18] To pray authentically, to live in union with the Word of God (*theologos*) is what Christian life means. Theology meant union with God and holiness of life issuing from that union long before it referred to academic study.[19] It is an activity for ordinary Christians, who will continue to ask fundamental questions. What is life all about? What does it mean to be human? What is the meaning of birth, of sexuality, of death? What is God doing in the events of the world? Ordinary Christians, ordinary people, do ask these questions. Theology is done at the street level. But does the Christian community provide a framework in which such questions make sense? Is it a place within which serious reflection, rooted in the real conflicts and struggles of the people, can take place? Is it a zone of truth, of discovery, of reality?

Theology is ordinary, and yet there is something extraordinary about theology in the present climate. For there is within our culture no framework of assumptions, of common wisdom and understanding, within which meaningful theological work can be done. Augustine, Aquinas and Calvin all wrote out of, and from within, a living tradition in which certain beliefs about the nature of the world and of the human person were assumed. This is no longer possible. The marginalisation of theology is therefore a cultural fact and a cultural necessity, and the longer we evade this the more desperate and incapable of resolution will our dilemma be. This is not pessimism, it is realism. To recover theology as a discipline of ordinary people and ordinary back street churches can only begin by recognising the extraordinary position of Christians, and indeed of all kinds of faith communities, in the contemporary climate.

Theology is a corporate activity which calls for the recovery of solitude. Yet our society has made both corporate identity and personal interiority more difficult. In their place we have the state and individuals, the realm of the political (increasingly reserved for professionals) and the realm of the private. But theology cannot exist without communities of faith, truth and struggle, and without the deeply personal exploration of solitude and prayer which is akin to the work of the poet and the artist. The work of discernment, of interrogation, of reflection, is both a corporate and a personal discipline. There is therefore a twofold task: the nurturing and strengthening of those small base communities – the parish in the historic sense – which form the primary fabric of Christian consciousness; and the guidance of persons into their own ground, their own inner space. The two most essential theological, and pastoral, tasks are community building and spiritual direction.

Theology, thirdly, is a critical questioning discipline and yet is one which is rooted in a tradition. Here there are two dangerous mistakes. One is to assume that theology is no more than the handing down of propositions from the past. The other is to assume that theology is something that we make up as we go along. It is not uncommon for people who start by holding the former view to end up believing the latter. Both views receive attention in the Fulton Lecture given by the Bishop of London, Graham Leonard, which attracted attention several years ago.[20] He argues that a 'new reformation' is in process which will divide Christians into those who see Christianity as a body of revealed truth which cannot be changed, and those who believe that it is a human construct, made up, revised from time to time, adapted to 'the spirit of the age'. But this is a caricature and represents a serious misunderstanding of the nature of the divisions in the Christian world. There are probably no Christians anywhere who believe that *everything* is unchangeable, just as there are none who accept that *nothing* has been 'revealed'. To divide

Christian groups and individuals in this way is unreal and irresponsible. Christian theology can only operate within a tradition of some kind. Creed, dogma, sacramental life and spiritual disciplines are the context of theological work. But traditions are not static: they embody conflict, doubt, questioning and struggle. Without these components a tradition decays into mere convention and ultimately death. I would want to reformulate Leonard's thesis, and suggest that the really critical division at the present time is between those Christians who believe that the gospel, the tradition and theology itself is a pre-packaged, final, unchangeable system; and those who believe that it is living, dynamic, and open to the future, to new insights, new understandings.

Finally, theology cannot be done by theologians alone, but it cannot be done without them. I would not wish to deny the importance of the serious systematic thinker within the Christian movement, but there has to be a living relationship, earthed and continuous, between the theologian and the communities in the back streets. At present they are hardly in touch. It is vital that we take seriously Antonio Gramsci's concept of the 'organic intellectual' and relate it to theology and the active Christian movement.[21]

One of the most serious problems for intellectuals, including theologians, is that the culture of academia encourages them to live at the level of ideas, at a 'head' level. But ideas do not exist independently of concrete social reality, and human beings are not heads but personalities in historical social formations. It is here, in a critique of, and a revolution in, intellectual and theological method, that we can see the relevance of liberation theology for Britain. For liberation theologians insist that the proof, the manifestation, and the justification of Christian faith is not intellectual but practical. In the words of Sharon Welch:

> The truth of Christian faith is at stake not in terms of its coherence with ontological structures and their potential modifications, but in life and death struggles, in daily operations of power/knowledge. It is in this arena of the

121

determination of the character of daily life that the truth of Christian faith, both in its method and referent, must be determined. The battle against nihilism and oppression is not primarily conceptual but practical. The focus therefore of a liberating faith and of theology is not primarily the analysis of human being and its possibilities but the creation of redeemed communities.[22]

How can this be done? Where are local communities of faith and struggle to be found? How can they be nourished? These are urgent theological questions to which theologians seem to give little attention.

Liberation theology and the back streets

There is a paradox here, for undoubtedly liberation theology is very much in fashion at present, at least in some Christian circles. Most people, inside and outside the churches, have never heard of it. But within the world of academia it is being studied as another subject. I am told that they are studying it in Oxbridge, though not to any noticeable extent. But all over the affluent, mainly white, theological power centres of North America, the large volumes which have been produced south of Mexico are being carefully studied, and responses by North American thinkers, including blacks and feminists, have been appearing for some time. It is not uncommon for Latin American theologians to be brought in as visiting professors at British and North American seminaries. In Britain, most theologians, not to mention the ecclesiastical bureaucracy, carry on as if nothing had happened. Yet even here one finds that the works of Gutierrez, Segundo, Miguez-Bonino, Sobrino and others, well-bound and looking like any other theological work, are displayed in very conservative bookshops such as SPCK and Mowbrays. Even the evangelical shops which do not stock 'unsound' authors will allow their customers to read what Andrew Kirk tells them about theology and revolution.[23]

Meanwhile, in the back streets, what does it all add up to? Has anything changed? The theological élites have found new things to discuss, and publishers new ways of making money. But the consumer society is very experienced at taking over new themes and movements, co-opting them, and selling them as commodities like anything else. Has liberation theology been co-opted as part of the establishment theological agenda? To pose the question in this way is, of course, simplistic and begs many questions about what co-option is, and the mechanics of academic publishing. One could ask the same question about Marx, feminism, racism, and so on. I do not mean any disrespect to liberation theologians by asking the question – not that disrespect from me is of any significance in the context of Third World oppression, rather I wish to suggest that there is a real danger that, to the extent that liberation issues have become part of the existing western theological agenda at all, they have only done so within the models of theology already accepted. Liberation theology has not been perceived as a revolution in method, in the way in which theology is practised, but has simply been added as an additional item to the existing theological curriculum. As such it is as irrelevant to what goes on in the back streets and among the common people as is any other item on that curriculum.

In the process of co-option the subversive power of the movement is eroded. Lectureships in liberation theology become as much a part of the academic cultural milieu as those in any other subject, and as disconnected with the realities of which they speak. Only the radical rhetoric survives, and is easily absorbed into the language of Christian liberalism. To that extent, for all his factual mistakes and carelessness, Edward Norman's polemic against much liberal Christianity is correct.[24] The process of preserving a radical sounding rhetoric as part of the vocabulary of the status quo is a well used method of taming potentially dangerous movements. It is precisely because the intellectual and ecclesiastical power structures – or some of them – have realised that liberation theology is threatening to their existence (and that is what the Boff dispute was really about) that they are concerned to take over some of the language and ideas, giving them an 'orthodox' stamp, while ignoring their meaning at every important point. Thus Pope John Paul II speaks of the need for 'a correct Christian idea of liberation'.[25] In his concern for the 'correct line', the Pope may be closer to some currents of Marxism than are the theologians whom he criticises.

Liberation theology is not about a correct, or an incorrect, idea of liberation: it is about liberation as a reality. In both the context of Latin America and of Britain, it is about a twofold liberation. On the one hand, it is an attempt to pursue the discipline of Christian theological reflection within the context of a commitment to the liberation of the oppressed and crushed peoples of the world. On the other, it is a recognition of the fact that it is not possible to pursue such a commitment without also seeking to end the present captivity of the church and of theology itself within the structures of oppression. There can be no theology of liberation without the liberation of theology. Christians who commit themselves to the struggle against structural oppression, embodied in the west in the structures of capitalism, will quickly find that in working against the capitalist system they are working also against the structures of the churches insofar as they are inextricably bound up with that system.

A theology of liberation is thus a partisan theology. It must decide where it stands in relation to the struggles of specific groups of oppressed people, and that decision cannot be taken ahistorically. In Britain it cannot be taken in isolation from the history of the working-class movement. Much 'radical' Christianity speaks of 'solidarity with the poor' or of 'bias to the poor' in a romantic way which seeks to relate to 'the poor' by bypassing the class structure. But a liberation theology for Britain will not make sense outside the context of the labour movement of the last hundred years. As far as the churches are concerned, this dimension of liberation must take its point of direction from those parts of the church which stand within, or are closely allied to, the labour movement. This is in no way to ignore the reactionary and blinkered features within the labour movement, but it is to recognise the crucial need for any liberation struggle to be a struggle which is rooted within and works alongside the movement of the working class as a whole.

The second theme of liberation theology is the liberation of theology itself, and of the church and the academic structures within which theology occurs. Here a distinction needs to be made between England, where academic theology in many places is in danger of becoming an extinct discipline,[26] and the United States where systematic theology and social ethics are major parts of most university curricula: and also between the churches, where what is called theology often amounts to no more than theoretical polemic in defence of positions which have already been adopted, and academia where the 'objective' study of religion is often pursued wholly unrelated to any life of prayer, discipleship or concern with social justice. I have argued above that, by its nature, liberation theology cannot simply be taken on by the existing academic enclaves, the 'antiseptic laboratories' to which Juan Luis Segundo refers.[27] Equally, as the 'second step' and as something which only 'arises at sundown',[28] liberation theology cannot be a prepackaged set of propositions which can be applied directly to any situation. Rather it is a continuing process of reflection on lived experience. The demand of liberation theology therefore is a demand for a revolution in the way in which theology happens.

However, when we relate these two aspects of liberation to Britain, a striking difference between Latin America and our situation is revealed. In Latin America, the Christian tradition, mainly but not exclusively in its Catholic form, provides a major resource for revolutionary struggle, and popular piety nourishes popular revolt. Because of this, liberation theology, and the history of the rebel church in Latin America, presents a major challenge to the classical Marxist view of religion as an opiate. But in the more secularised society of Britain, it is not at all clear that Christianity, or indeed any form of religion, can provide such impetus and nourishment.

There are, of course, important exceptions: the Irish liberation struggle and its roots in Catholic radicalism; the growing radicalisation of the independent black churches; the potential appeal of Islam to many young Asians; the growth of Rastafarianism as a kind of street liberation tradition; the feminist movement inside and outside the main church structures; and so on. But for the most part the white working class – and increasingly the black working class – is much more alienated from organised religion of all kinds than is the case in Latin America. The Church of England may be more 'liberal' at its official level than either the Vatican or the Latin American hierarchies. But that may mean little more than that a rebel tradition, a 'subversive church', is less likely to arise here. The genteel liberalism of the institution may actually be a major barrier against any genuine liberation theology for Britain. As one legendary MP is alleged to have exclaimed during a parliamentary debate: 'For heaven's sake, hands off the Church of England. It's the only thing that stands between us and Christianity'.

It seems likely then that a Christian liberation tradition will not occur at the level of the British working class (to whom for the most part, the Christian tradition, as mediated by successive generations of churches, is essentially alien) or at the level of the ecclesiastical 'corridors of power' (to whom liberation theology is a theme for pious reflection, not a serious option). It is more likely to occur among the marginalised elements within, and on the edge of, both camps. I want therefore to return to the question of marginality with which I began this book.

Marginality has generally been viewed within most sections both of the church and of the left as the road to the wilderness, to isolation, to futility. By retaining one's ideological or spiritual purity at the cost of practical relevance, the radical Christian or the revolutionary socialist is portrayed as having opted for witness and vision over against effectiveness. Yet when George Orwell described Anglo-Catholicism as the ecclesiastical version of Trotskyism,[29] he actually hit upon more than he realised. For it was within such movements as the Catholic

126

Crusade that a rebel tradition within Anglicanism arose with close similarities to the liberation theology of the present day. Yet like Trotskyism the culture of Anglo-Catholicism became increasingly marked by archaism and unreality. Duncan Hallas's description of 'orthodox' Trotskyism could be applied, with a few simple word changes, both to Anglo-Catholicism and to other tendencies within the Christian movement

> They constituted a tendency characterised by theoretical primitiveness and conservatism, by a marked reluctance to depart from the letter of Trotsky's writings, which, at times, they elevated almost to the status of sacred texts. Consequently their world outlook came to diverge more and more from reality.[30]

As such it was easy for both the church as a whole and the socialist movement as a whole to regard these groups as at best tiresome nuisances and at worst utterly irrelevant survivals. But this was far from correct.

The history of radical Christianity in Britain and elsewhere has often been portrayed in terms of irrelevant sectarian visionaries. The word 'utopian' is often used about them. Yet that history includes such significant groups as the Catholic radicals who led the 1381 rising;[31] the apocalyptic radicals of the seventeenth century – Diggers, Levellers, Fifth Monarchy men and so on;[32] the Anglican socialists who emerged from the post–1870 period;[33] the Catholic anarchism of Dorothy Day and Peter Maurin in the USA;[34] and the black Christian tradition which has played such an important part in combating racism in the USA and elsewhere.[35] What these groups have offered is an alternative vision of what Christianity is or could be, and they have kept that vision alive in apparently hopeless periods. They have nourished a culture of rebellion and helped others to create a new history out of the old.

The original Christian marginal rebel movement was that of the fourth-century desert monks. In their retreat into the desert at the time of the beginnings of the 'Constantinian establishment' of Christianity, they kept alive the vision of the new age through the centuries of darkness. The Constantinian era is now at an end, and the emergence of liberation theology is one aspect of its collapse, just as the right-wing 'Christian Reconstructionism' in the USA is a final attempt to restore it.[36] The next few decades are likely therefore to see the emergence of minority 'confessing churches' similar to that which helped to lead the resistance to Hitler. Such groups would need to build upon the rebel tradition within historic Christianity. They might provide a major focus for the liberation of theology.

But such groups alone would be little more than Christian élites unless there was a well-recognised and continuous engagement with the socialist movement and with the growing numbers of people who are alienated from all organised structures, religious and political. There is abundant evidence in Britain today of the growth of a new 'underclass', of increasing and shifting groups of rootless, marginal people. It is no longer adequate to regard such groups as *lumpen*. It is likely that out of this culture a movement similar to that of Latin American liberation theology will arise: in fact evidence suggests that it is already in existence. Unlike Latin America it is not a movement inspired directly by Christianity, nor does it fit easily within the traditional thought forms of the left. It is itself a product of capitalism in its most developed and most cruel phase. Confronted by the most clear evidence of an upsurge of racism, intolerance and attacks on minorities in Europe since the time of Hitler, it is essential that the rebel groups within and on the edge of the churches, secular socialists, and the movements of the oppressed who form the new underclass in the cities find ways of uniting and working together. In such a process of collaboration, the Christian rebel tradition may well rediscover its identity and essential comradeship with many people outside its borders, and this could be a truly liberating experience and perhaps the beginning of a new phase of struggle. For the acid test of the relevance of liberation theology for Britain is whether it has anything to offer to the neglected, broken, angry, and forgotten people of the back streets.

Subversive orthodoxy: the growth of the Jubilee Group

It was out of the sense of need for a street theology that the Jubilee Group arose towards the end of 1974. All we originally had in mind was a support group for people who seemed to be working and thinking along similar lines. The group has changed in major ways since then, but a brief account of its emergence may be a useful case study of one attempt to combine a reflective theology with the pursuit of social struggle.

The Jubilee Group began as a small group of priests in the East End of London in October 1974. I had been instituted as Rector of St Matthew's Church, Bethnal Green, on 21 September, and a few weeks later I sent a letter to a number of friends suggesting that we might form a support group for one another. We had in common the fact that we were all priests who stood broadly within the Catholic tradition of Anglicanism; we were all socialists of some kind; and we were all involved in active ministry, mainly in the East End, particularly concerned with such areas as race, homelessness, unemployment, youth work, and so on. But in addition we were all deeply unhappy at the state of the Anglo-Catholic movement in the Church of England. I wrote:

> A number of us are very disturbed at the trend in the Catholic movement towards a sickly pietism and a right-wing reactionary stance in social and political issues. This trend represents a serious betrayal of the social tradition of Anglo-Catholicism and it may represent the death of the movement as such. Whether the present organs of Anglo-Catholic opinion are reformable remains to be seen: it is hardly likely that any of them will be transformed into organs of revolutionary zeal. They seem to be more concerned with changes in the liturgy than with changes in the world, and one fears that for too many within the Catholic movement, religion has become a substitute for life.

It is fascinating to read those words over fifteen years later.

At the time some people criticised the use of the word 'trend', pointing out that the sickly pietism had always been there since the beginning of the movement. We were undoubtedly naive in thinking that there was a single 'social tradition' to which we could appeal and which had been betrayed, and many of us have come to see that the whole cluster of practices and ideas which has become known as Anglo-Catholicism contains complex and conflicting elements.[36] Nevertheless at the time many of us did think in terms of some kind of 're-calling' to a lost tradition, some kind of 'renewal' of the Catholic movement, and it was with this in mind that Jubilee moved from being a support group to being a pressure group within the Anglo-Catholic movement.

My own sense of the need for some kind of 'Catholic renewal' movement went back some years. As long ago as 1961 I had been involved with Gresham Kirkby, parish priest of St Paul's, Bow Common, in forming a group called the 'Catholic Revival' Group. Nothing came of this, but the idea continued to germinate. It was expressed in a sermon which I preached in Canterbury Cathedral in 1973 (see Appendix 3). Though I did not realise it at the time, this sermon was probably the beginning of the Jubilee Group in my mind. On the other hand, in spite of our romantic and naive hopes for a renewal of the tradition, there was an ominous line in my letter which was to be an omen for the future. I suggested that the movement might be close to death. That sentence was to prove more prophetic than other more positive parts of the letter.

Jubilee in its origins was white, male and clerical. After a few years it ceased to be so, and its transformation is more exciting and more significant than its origins. Yet, even with these limitations, we did recognise that there was a need for active Christians at the local level to practise theological reflection within the social and political context of their work. We were deliberately and consciously not a group of aca-demics, and we were very explicitly a group who stood within the socialist movement. It was within this context of activism and political commitment that we sought to make theological

130

and prayerful sense of our work in the East End and elsewhere.

By November 1974 the group had grown and had spread to other parts of London, Oxford, and the West Midlands. Some members in Oxford drafted a manifesto. It was written very quickly in an Oxford pub, was never adopted by the group as a whole, and was felt by many to be hopelessly triumphalist. Yet it did express some of the frustration as well as the passion that was about at this time.

'Our social programme is the dogma of the Holy Trinity' (Nikolai Fyodorov). We are committed to the struggle for justice, liberty and peace, not because of some secondary interest in social theory, but because of the very foundation of the Catholic faith. We believe that humanity is made in the image of the Triune God, and is therefore social; that in Christ humanity is restored to its full capacity for social being. We believe that humanity is called to share the life of the Holy Trinity, the life of love and communion. We cannot therefore feign neutrality or remain uncritical in the face of a society based upon the ruthless pursuit of private gain and unlimited consumption. The institutionalised egotism of all forms of capitalism, including its Soviet collectivised form, must be challenged by Catholic Christians, if we are to remain faithful to the whole gospel of Christ.

'The doctrine of the incarnation is the announcement of a divine gift conveyed in a material and visible medium, it being thus that heaven and earth are in the incarnation united. That is, it establishes in the very idea of Christianity the sacramental principle as its characteristic' (Newman). Our sacramental vision liberates us from enslavement, both by sickly pietism and by human ideologies, and brings us into a living relationship with history. We see an immediate and necessary connection between the sacrament of the altar and the 'sacrament of the brother' (St John Chrysostom). Catholic Christianity believes in the Real Presence of Christ, not only in the Eucharist but also in the least of his brothers and sisters. Because our fathers in the Catholic

131

movement worshipped Christ in the sacrament, they also loved, cared for, and identified with him in the wretched of the earth. Moreover they saw that their sacramentalism struck a blow against the idolatry of profit, power and privilege, of imperialism and racial domination. They knew that Christ whom they received in the sacrament cleanses his temple of all injustice and exploitation.

What they said in Victorian and Edwardian England we must proclaim in our situation today. Our commitment to the struggle of the oppressed must be as passionate as theirs. For, while much has changed over the last hundred years, the poor still starve throughout the Third World and in the streets of our cities.

We are 'subversive contemplatives'. We are not shallow activists. What makes us revolutionary is our prayer, the heart of our Christian life. Our 'union with the Father leads us, in a sense charged with legal jeopardy, to resistance against false, corrupting, coercive imperialist policy' (Daniel Berrigan). Our prayer is our ultimate rejection of the aims, assumptions, structures and institutions of a world organised apart from Christ. As we grow in conformity to him, as we live more and more to the Lord and not to self, we find ourselves moving in opposition to the enforcement of all those pseudo-values fostered by capitalism.

We do not run away from history. We know what the present crisis of capitalism demands of us. We must, above all, revive the prophetical office of the church. Now that we are in the death-throes of late capitalism, which threatens to inflict even greater violence on humanity than it has done before, we must make our stand with the oppressed, with the movement for liberation throughout the world. Only so far can we be true to Christ, his Gospel and his Catholic Church.

This 1974 manifesto contains much that is naive and romantic, and parts of it cause us some embarrassment when we re-read it in the climate of the 1990s. Yet the underlying

theology is sound, and the responses to its circulation brought
it home to us that there was an increasing number of people
in very diverse Christian traditions – Roman Catholics influenced by liberation theology, Mennonites, radical evangeli-
cals, Quakers, Methodists, as well as the socialist wing of
Anglo-Catholicism – who were thinking and feeling along
similar lines. In a modest way Jubilee helped to bring many
of them together to discover and explore common ground.
Clearly a new movement was stirring within, and on the edge
of, the churches. Soon the very name Jubilee (which we had
innocently taken from Leviticus 25 with its vision of equality
and freedom within a common land) started to be used by
Christians of rather differing outlooks but all sharing a social
commitment.

For some time Jubilee remained a clerical, Anglo-Catholic
socialist grouping, though it soon ceased to be an exclusively
East End group. There was probably never any conscious
wish to restrict the group to priests. It was more that, having
started in this way, we did not have the will, or the consciousness of the need, to take 'affirmative action' and open it to
non-clerics. That came later. Some accused us of being too
narrowly tied to one wing of the church. Yet most of us felt
in those early years that there was a very specific task to be
done in relation to the Anglo-Catholic movement (or what
was left of it), and this task did seem to call for a fairly narrow
base if it was to work. We spoke of 'recalling the movement
to its lost traditions'. It was later that we began to gather
people who were neither socialists nor Anglo-Catholics but
had some kind of broad sympathy with what we were saying.
While we have always described ourselves as a network of
socialist Christians who stand mainly within the Catholic
tradition of Anglicanism, we have never excluded people who
cannot identify with this position *in toto*, and we have many
fellow-travellers who are neither socialists nor Christians but
who find in Jubilee a supportive and stimulating atmosphere.

A leaflet from 1975 expressed our general position.

The Group came into being as result of a series of

discussions on the current state of Catholicism in the Church of England. While there were, and are, some important differences among us, we found that we were united in (1) a commitment to the Catholic movement, and a strong sense of standing within the tradition of Catholic Orthodoxy; (2) a sense of alarm and frustration at the present decayed and demoralised state of the movement; and (3) a concern for the resurrection of the unity of contemplation and politics. In addition, within the wider framework of Christianity, we shared (4) a concern at the woolly liberalism of much current social action in the church and in particular at the state of the 'Christian Left' with its lack of clear theological thought.

Since its beginnings, Jubilee has changed to a remarkable degree. It is still very much a support group, loosely organised – at times so loosely that people doubt whether it exists at all. Local groups rise and fall according to needs in particular districts. For some, it has become a way of keeping in touch with like-minded people in other parts of the country, for others it plays the role of a very localised group to stimulate and to throw around ideas. A network or 'tendency' rather than an organisation. Jubilee has tried to create an environment within which Christians on the left can support, learn from, argue with, and nurture one another. Most of its members are activists, heavily involved in the struggles and upheavals of society, and who feel the need for a reflective group within which they can do theology. It remains small, it has serious weaknesses, and it is a frustratingly messy network. Yet in spite of all these faults, it holds out a hope for a future in which theology and life, contemplation and action, prayer and politics, mystics and militants can be more integrated and thus more effective instruments of the Kingdom of God.[37]

A faith for the city

These pastoral reflections have been rooted in the context of
the city. In the gospels, Jesus weeps over the city of Jerusalem
because it does not know 'the things that make for peace'
(Luke 19:41–2). My ministry in the city has not been exactly
peaceful, and the years that I have discussed are marked, it
would seem, by conflict rather than by peace. In fact modern
cities, from the beginnings of industrialisation, have rarely
been seen as centres of peace, but rather of upheaval, turmoil
and suffering. The very language of urban studies is filled
with what Ruth Glass has termed 'verbal incendiary devices':
exploding cities, the urban time bomb, and so on. A whole
series of Pavlovian reactions to words has grown up in current
urban jargon. So 'urban' suggests 'crisis' or 'conflict'. 'Inner
city' suggests 'problem'. Even the word 'street' cannot, it
seems, now be used in a straightforward way. In 1986, in a
report on the church and racism, some of us urged the Church
of England to get 'out of the committee room and on to the
streets',[38] a fairly clear way, we thought, of stressing the need
for less concern with committees and more involvement with
ordinary people. This was too much for one Conservative
MP, described as a 'leading member of the Church of
England', who, a day or so before the report had been distrib-
uted and a week before it was published, said: 'This report
advocates activists taking to the streets and causing turmoil'.[39]
So 'street' – the place where most people live, move and have
their being – has now, in the right-wing mind, become a
synonym for disorder, riot and violence.

Christians are not immune from this tradition of urban
demonology. We have contributed to a view of the city as
intrinsically, irredeemably evil, a God-forsaken place. I
believe that we need to repent of, and renounce, such views
of the city, and to witness to the truth that God is at work in
cities as much as in the countryside and the suburbs where
the church is more at home. That does not mean that we
romanticise urban life or pretend that nothing is wrong. It
does mean that we have faith in the city, hope for the city,

and love of the city as the place, for thousands of people, where the encounter with God and with the demands of the Kingdom must take place. In the New Testament the city is the place of crucifixion and of resurrection. So we need to exercise our ministry in the city as a community which seeks peace, and seeks to be a community of peacemakers. We need to ask: what are 'the things that belong to peace' and how do they connect with the faith which we are called to preach and live?

Peace, *shalom*, means more in Jewish and Christian thought than the absence of war and conflict, and more than a state of inner calm. In Hebrew it means wholeness, completeness. It is closely akin to salvation itself (Judg. 8:9–1; 1 Kgs. 22:27–8; Prov. 12:20; Ps. 37: 37; Lev. 26:1–13). It depends upon justice: there can be no peace for the wicked (Isa. 48:22). Peace in the biblical record includes material provisions and bodily health as well as harmony and non-violence (Ps. 28:3; 73:3; Judg. 19:20f). 'They shall not hurt or destroy in all my holy mountain. . .' (Mi. 4:1–4; Isa. 2:2–4). This passage links the practice of non-violence and of cooperation within a society of equals with the knowledge of the Lord. It is a vision of a new society towards which we struggle.

For peace is not seen in the prophetic writings as an inevitable state. it has to be struggled for, worked for. Zechariah speaks of 'a sowing of peace' (Zech. 8:12). In the gospels, the stress on the need to *make* peace is continued: it is the peace*makers*, not simply the peace*ful*, who are the children of God (Matt. 5:9). So peace is both a gift and a goal: peace is given to us so that we may struggle for its manifestation in the world and in our local neighbourhoods. Elsewhere in the New Testament peace is the fruit of justification (Rom. 5:1), as one of the fruits of the Spirit (Gal. 5:22), one of the characteristics of the presence of the Kingdom of God (justice and peace and joy in the Holy Spirit, Rom. 14:17.) Christ himself is described as our peace (Eph. 2:14), God is the God of peace (Rom. 15:33; 16:20; 2 Cor. 13:11; Phil. 4:9; 1 Thess. 5:23; Heb. 13:20), our hearts and our minds are to be kept

136

in the peace of God (Phil. 4:7). 'Peace be with you' is one of the oldest Christian greetings.

Peace is a particularly important theme in Luke where the word *eirene* is used fourteen times (in contrast to once in Mark and four times in Matthew). Significantly in Luke's understanding, peace is associated with the enlightenment of the nations (Luke 1: 79; 2:32). Luke 'clearly dissociates *eirene* from any restrictive personalistic meaning in which peace is a matter of the heart or only an individual and merely personal experience. *Eirene* is associated with relation and structural realities'.[40]

On the other hand, in both Old and New Testaments, there is a false peace. Jeremiah and Ezekiel attack those who cry 'Peace, peace' when there is no peace (Jer. 6:14; 8:11; Ez. 13:10). Amos cries 'Woe to those who are at ease in Zion' (Amos 6:1), those who enjoy peace and security in the midst of injustice and oppression. In the gospels, Jesus warns his hearers that he has not come to bring peace. 'Do you think that I have come to bring peace on earth? No, I tell you, but rather division.' (Luke 12:51).

So, paradoxically, the proclamation of the gospel of peace is associated with the creation of turbulence as the gospel comes into conflict with what the New Testament terms 'the world'. In our own day the gospel is bound to collide and conflict with the values and assumptions of a society geared to a war economy, a society where profits matter more than people, a society based on the worship and service of Mammon, and on the maintenance of structures of oppression. In such a society, the proclamation of the gospel of peace becomes a subversive activity. Yet my experience is that the churches do not welcome such conflict. A superficial peace and harmony have come to be valued more than the pursuit of truth and justice with all its hazardous consequences. Yet this pursuit is the only way to the authentic peace which is that of biblical faith.

Peace then is the end to which the gospel directs us, and the end which we seek for the city. What are the conditions?

What kind of faith is it which must be preached and lived if the city is to experience *shalom*?

First, it must be a faith which offers freedom. Freedom, liberation, redemption: these words – all in fact the same word – are basic to the biblical record, from the demand of Moses 'Let my people go!' (Ex. 5:1; 7:16; 8:1, 20; 9:1, 13; 10:3) to Paul's assertion 'You were called to freedom' (Gal. 5:13). The faith of the Bible is obsessed with the theme of freedom.

But our proclamation of gospel freedom has been reduced to a proclamation of freedom from personal sin. That freedom is important: personal liberation is essential. But it is not enough. The gospel of Christian freedom goes beyond the personal realm. It sets persons free from all forms of bondage: from slavery to unjust oppressors, from the principalities and powers, the rulers of the darkness of this world, and so on. According to Paul in Romans 8, it is not only persons who are liberated: the creation itself will be set free from bondage to enjoy the freedom of the children of God. So Christian freedom is a total freedom. Christ, by his cross and resurrection, has set us free from the captivity to all earthly powers, set us free to serve only God and his Kingdom.

But the city is a place of bondage and oppression for many. It is not a zone of liberation. It is not a place where men and women experience the liberating word of the gospel. The church, instead of being a community set free by the gospel, set free to confront and to challenge the principalities and powers, has become enslaved to them, and has become a church conformed to the world. There is a Babylonian captivity of the churches: they have sold out to the fallen world order, and so I believe that there must be a liberation of the church itself from its entanglement with injustice and oppression. There is, as Jim Wallis tells us, a clear choice between established religion and biblical faith.[41]

There is another sense in which faith must set people free. It must free people from blindness, from the slavery of not seeing what is going on. A religion which blurs vision, which produces glazed eyes, which prevents us from seeing clearly,

138

is not a biblical faith and is not a liberating faith. A faith which does not set people free from bondage, a faith which is not liberating faith, is a faith which can offer nothing to the city except comfort in the midst of affliction.

Secondly, faith must proclaim and pursue justice. Justice, like freedom, is a key biblical word and concept. In the prophets, to do justice is to know the Lord (Jer. 22:15–16). Without the pursuit of justice, worship is blasphemous and insulting to God. I believe that we need to recover this prophetic faith, the faith which pursues justice. The neglect of the Old Testament has had extremely damaging consequences for the church. Karl Barth once commented that had the churches in Germany paid as much attention to the Old Testament prophets as they did to Romans 13, the history of the Nazi period might have been quite different.[42] Today it is essential that we recover the heart of that Jewish materialist and historical faith if we are to minister adequately in the cities of Britain.

This prophetic faith has clear consequences for those who pursue and maintain injustice and oppression, and I believe that inner-city pastors are under a biblical mandate to draw attention to the prophetic word as a word of judgement for the powerful today. Take, for instance, the words of Amos:

For three transgressions of Israel and for four, I will not revoke the punishment, because they sell the righteous for silver and the needy for a pair of shoes – they that trample the head of the poor into the dust of the earth and turn aside the way of the afflicted (Amos 2:6–7.)

Or Isaiah:

What do you mean by crushing my people, by grinding the faces of the poor? says the Lord of hosts. (Isa. 3:15.)

And again:

Woe to those who decree iniquitous decrees, and the writers who keep writing oppression, to turn aside the needy from

139

justice, and to rob the poor of my people of their right. . .
(Isa. 10:1–2).

We need to relate these biblical warnings to our situation in
the modern city. Andrew Kirk, whilst in the process of writing
a book on contemporary political issues, asked himself: how
would the prophet Amos have responded? And he wrote as
follows:

> Hear, oh countries of the western world, this word of the
> Lord: you sell the righteous for silver and the needy for a
> pair of shoes (marked 'made in Brazil'). You trample the
> heads of the poor into the dust of the earth and turn aside
> the way of the afflicted. You take exactions from the poor
> (copper from Chile and Zambia, tin from Bolivia, coffee
> from Uganda, tea from Sri Lanka, fish from Peru.) You
> have built houses of hewn stone (and filled them with trivial
> luxuries). Therefore it shall be night to you without vision;
> the seers (economic advisers) shall be disgraced and the
> diviners (those who use biblical prophecy to justify the self-
> interest of their country) shall be put to shame. There is
> no answer from God.[43]

The pastor in the city has a clear biblical mandate, and an
obligation under pain of mortal sin, to condemn injustice and
to warn those in power of the consequences of their actions.
In Scripture, the issue of how the poor, the alien, the orphan
and the widow are treated is a clear spiritual criterion of the
spiritual health of any society. As Jim Wallis has written:

> That God is on the side of the poor, and that the Scriptures
> are uncompromising in their demand for economic and
> social justice is much more clear biblically than are most
> of the issues over which churches have divided. The Scrip-
> tures claim that to know God is to do justice and to plead
> the cause of the oppressed. Yet this central biblical impera-
> tive is one of the first to be purged from a church that has
> conformed and made accommodations to the established
> order.[44]

I believe, thirdly, that faith must be a force for reconciliation. The truth that God was in Christ reconciling the world to himself is a vital aspect of the Christian gospel. Equally important is the truth, expressed in the same passage (2 Cor. 5:18–19), that God has entrusted to us both the message (*logos*) and the ministry (*diakonia*) of reconciliation. However, I believe that there are two serious dangers in the way that Christians are inclined to use the notion of reconciliation.

The first relates to the biblical teaching. It is possible to exaggerate the importance of the language of reconciliation in the New Testament. The words 'reconciliation' and 'reconcile' do not in fact occur much in the New Testament. Reconciliation is only one way in which the work of salvation is described. Only Paul uses these words in relation to the gospel.[45] If we isolate reconciliation with God from other dimensions of biblical teaching, we can end up with a very one-sided and individualistic view of salvation. We need, for example, to attend also to the teaching of Ephesians about the breaking down of the wall of partition, and to that of Galatians about liberation from slavery.

There is a second danger in the language of reconciliation. It is easy to misuse this language as a way of bypassing both the demands of justice (without which reconciliation, like peace, is a sham) and the inevitability of conflict. The immediate result of the preaching of Jesus was not reconciliation. Take, for example, the Nazareth sermon in Luke 4 in which Jesus announces release to captives and the recovery of sight to the blind. He proclaims the Year of Jubilee. Yet what is the response to this preaching? 'When they heard all this, all in the synagogue were filled with wrath. And they rose up and put him out of the city, and led him to the brow of the hill on which their city was built that they might throw him down headlong' (Luke 4:18–9). Jesus' preaching did not immediately reconcile. Indeed the only people who are described in the gospels as being reconciled as a result of the preaching of Jesus are Herod and Pilate (Luke 23:12)!

Today, however, we are constantly being told, not least by bishops, that the church's social role is one of reconciliation.

I want seriously to question this. The church's primary role is to proclaim the truth, to seek justice, and to plead the cause of the oppressed, all within the framework of the worship of God. That may lead to reconciliation, but it seems very unlikely: it is more likely, on the historical evidence, to lead to anger and division. But without truth, justice and the concern for the poor, reconciliation is simply a euphemism for acquiescence in oppression. It is the comfortable message of those who are at ease in Zion. In the memorable words of the late Saul Alinsky, 'Reconciliation means I am in power and you get reconciled to it'.[46]

In case I am misunderstood, let me stress that I am not in any way denying that reconciliation is the long-term goal of the Christian, as indeed it is of all who seek a just and peaceful world. But it cannot and must not be the immediate aim. If it is it will certainly be reconciliation at the expense of truth, justice and the defence of the poor. It is those imperatives which must come first.

Fourthly, faith must offer healing and wholeness of life. In the gospel, the cleansing of lepers, the healing of the lame, and the enlightening of the blind are among the signs of the Kingdom of God. And today, wherever human beings and human communities make steps towards wholeness of life, shaking off the burden of crippling and enslaving powers, there God is at work, there the Kingdom is present. Our faith is a faith which is concerned with the healing and transformation of individuals and communities so that they come to reflect the image of God and the life of the city of God.

A faith which does justice to urban needs cannot be one which adopts fundamentally negative positions towards individual and social transformation, and this has, I believe, two important consequences. First, it means recognising that human beings are not simply fallen creatures. They are images of God, made for God's glory. We need therefore to recover the stress on sanctification as the transfiguring of human nature, and to reject the over-emphasis on the fall which fails to treat seriously the transforming power of grace. Secondly, it means recognising that the earth, the nations, the city, the life of the back streets, are not doomed: they are the site of sanctification. The earth is to be filled with the glory of God.

We need, therefore to rethink our attitudes to 'the world' and to what we understand as 'worldliness'. The New Testament combines both an acceptance and joyful celebration of the world, meaning the created earth, as made, loved, redeemed and sustained by God; and a renunciation of the world, meaning the fallen world order and its false value systems. Christian people are called not to be conformed but to be transformed (Rom. 12:2), and to be instruments of transformation within the world. It is all too easy to get this wrong, and to combine a false otherworldliness in theology with a very compromised worldliness in practice.

Finally, faith must be the faith of the Kingdom of God. The good news of the Kingdom of God, the heart of the gospel, is the truth that God is mending his broken creation, and our task is to recognise, and then to cooperate with, this activity of God. It is a work which must be done in minute particulars, for the Kingdom is built brick by brick. It is a work for the freedom of humankind and of the creation. It is a work for justice, for peoples and nations. It is a work which brings reconciliation and peace, though there will be tribulation and struggle on the way. It is a work of transformation, for the Christian vision is of a transformed creation, a renewed and transfigured creation of which the risen Christ is the first fruits. It is a vision of new heavens and a new earth, where justice shall dwell (2 Peter 3:13), which will sustain our faith in the city.

Hope for the future?

It is twenty-one years since I opened up the disused basement at St Anne's Church in Soho, cleared out the cockroaches and the beetles, and started Centrepoint. Those who came through our doors in the first few months were in the main young people in search of work: they saw London as the source of hope. Many of them rapidly became hopeless, and their hopelessness was rooted in the recognition of a truth: that they were not needed, that their work and their lives were dispensable. They were of no value in what was later to become known as the enterprise culture.

To look back on those years is in many ways a deeply depressing experience, for since then the problems of homelessness, of economic poverty, of drug abuse as a consequence of despair, and of the alienation of large numbers of young people, have grown much, much worse, and to a degree that few of us foresaw at that time. The action to respond to these cries of hopelessness has been in almost inverse relationship to the degree of documentation about them. We know more today about homelessness, poverty and urban deprivation than we have ever known in recorded urban history. Every week new books and reports on poverty come out: they get more expensive by the week. Yet, even using the government data, the numbers of people living below or on the edge of the poverty line go on rising, and with that rise comes a rise in the level of despair. Christian pastors in the deprived areas often feel, like the prophet Zechariah, that they have become the shepherds of a flock doomed to slaughter (Zech. 11:4).

The increase in homelessness, both among families and single people, was well documented in the 1960s, not least by the groups around our own work in Soho and the links with the decline in privately rented housing, the maldistribution of housing in cities and the 'drift to the south' were all described then. Since then we have seen the increased movement of people from north to south in desperate search of work, and recent economic projections suggest that this will increase further, adding to the numbers of homeless people in the south. In the 1960s the drift was discouraged: today we have the 'get on your bike' philosophy, but those young people who follow that advice are then punished for doing so under the social security regulations. The increase in homelessness is paralleled by a far greater increase in poverty. Conservative estimates now put the figure around thirteen million. It is not surprising that the increased availability of

144

illicit heroin, classically the drug of despair, has led to the emergence of large addict communities in Merseyside, Glasgow, and Dublin, areas substantially unaffected in the 60s.

One of the most disturbing aspects of recent changes has been the 'racialisation' of poverty in some areas. So we now hear a good deal about the 'urban underclass', a euphemism for poor black people,[47] and what we hear corresponds to reality. For while it is true that many black people have made significant progress in British society, it is beyond doubt that poverty and unemployment have become increasingly allied with racial segregation and racial disadvantage. A large community of black poor has grown up in cities such as London, Birmingham, Manchester and Liverpool. Not that racism alone has created poverty: but it has added to it a new and vicious dimension, and it begins at the doors of Britain, in the clear message enshrined in legislation since 1962, that black people constitute a problem *per se*.

Racism cannot be accepted at the doors of Britain, and outlawed within Britain. Today, after nearly thirty years of racist immigration laws, racism is more gentrified, more acceptable, more respectable than it has been for a long time. At every point prejudice has been encouraged; compromise has replaced principle; and the earlier positive trends have been reversed. Rarely have tolerance, justice and equality been recognised as positive virtues to be struggled for as part of a real moral and political commitment. Nor is it simply a question of colour discrimination: a whole culture of bigotry and intolerance against minorities of all kinds has been created, and the sense of hopelessness has spread.

Perhaps the worst aspect of the recent increase in hopelessness is the apparent futility of talking about it to those who wield power in white society. For not only has the gulf between rich and poor grown; the gulf between government and people has assumed dimensions so great that one might be talking to people on Mars. Perhaps for the first time since the Second World War we have a government whose experience of life is so narrow and who are so protected from the problems that afflict the poor that incomprehension and

145

unreality have now become the norm rather than the exception. So hopelessness leads to a kind of social autism, an inability to effect change, a real paralysis of the spirit of which Ezekiel's valley of dry bones and Zechariah's image of a flock doomed to slaughter are the most fitting biblical symbols.

The level of anger and frustration has increased, of course, not least among those Christians who live and work in the urban cores, and whose view of reality differs fundamentally from that of the present regime. This is not because they are 'left' rather than 'right' or because they have not studied 'the facts', but because they are standing in a different place, and see a different reality – a reality from which comfortable Britain, encouraged by the government, averts its eyes.

This is all a very gloomy way to end a book, and yet I believe that there is no hope, and no future, in avoiding the gloom and the despair. I believe that the renewal of hope and of vision can only come on the basis of honest facing of the current reality. Hope cannot be rooted in illusion. To accept the complacent Thatcherite myth of an ever-increasing prosperity is to commit the mortal sin of bearing false witness. To face the seriousness of despair and hopelessness is the only way by which hope can be restored and a new vision discovered, and that honesty is a necessary part of our duty to the oppressed. To speak smooth words, to reassure, to trivialise the pain of despair and hopelessness, is an act of great cruelty and contempt towards people without hope. As the Latin American theologian Jon Sobrino has written: 'To stand before the poor with honesty is a first step in the humanisation of the human being'.[48]

Here we encounter a very serious problem which is usually avoided, particularly in church circles. It is the problem of how we witness, with any degree of integrity and credibility, to the equality of human beings in a church like the Church of England whose entire history is so involved with inequality, hierarchy and the maintenance of class divisions. I would not say it is impossible, and I remain an Anglican of sorts, albeit increasingly very much on the margins of the institution. But I believe that such a witness must fly in the face of so much

146

Anglican history that it can only be sustained within a subversive movement. And here those who cry 'A church in danger!' are actually correct, though perhaps not in the way they realise or could possibly understand. For a serious movement to end the age of oppression and create a more equal and more human society would undoubtedly mean the end of the Church of England as we know it.

What I am suggesting is that a genuine commitment to human dignity and to the cause of the crushed and the broken must move beyond the level of rhetoric, including the rhetoric of service and compassion. To serve and to show compassion are commendable characteristics, but they are no substitute for solidarity, for comradeship, for the unremitting determination to stand by the poor at the level of equality and shared struggle, and that means a struggle for a radically different society in which wealth and power are shared, in which the poor and lowly are given their dignity.

Here we meet a second major problem for the church, and this lies in its timidity, its fear of the state, its conformity to the values and norms of Caesar. Since the time of Constantine in the fourth century, the church has tended to ally itself with the established order: it has been a political church, and its politics have been the politics of the status quo. But that age is over. The Constantinian era has ended, and we are, as MacIntyre argues, in a new Dark Age. But, whereas in the first Dark Age, the barbarians were on the frontier, today they are in our midst and have been ruling us for some time.[49] The role of the church in this situation is not to help preserve the culture of barbarism but rather to help to build a counter-culture of resistance, an alternative network of communities within which human dignity and spiritual values can be preserved, communities which will outlast the present evil order.

The disentanglement of the church from the culture of oppression and of Mammon is a necessary preliminary to the renewal of its vision. Christians are not called to be servants of the state but rather its conscience and a witness to it that it stands under judgement. In the present crisis the role of the church is not to go on and on about the rule of law but to warn of judgement on those who grind the faces of the poor and to seek out and minister to the victims of cruelty and neglect. It is to celebrate with Mary the putting down of the mighty from their thrones and the exaltation of the poor and lowly, and to work for that vision to become a reality. It is to help nourish a culture of resistance and to renew and strengthen that rebel tradition which has always existed within the Christian movement.

The work of prophecy always begins with judgement, with woe, with the bad news. Only then can we move towards a new age of justice. And that process will be one marked by conflict and suffering. Hope is always hope 'in spite of . . .', it is never a gradual and genteel ascent towards utopia. It is always a process of dying and rising. Hope begins in darkness and dereliction, and it is out of this darkness and dereliction that the word of God speaks to us. He is risen. The culture of death and oppression is not the end. Babylon is falling. It is out of its ruins that the new age will be born.

The Christian hope is the hope of a new age. It is a hope which involves our commitment and our effective mobilisation. It is a hope, but more than a hope: it is a reality rooted in the facts of Christ's incarnation, death and resurrection, and in the power of the Spirit-filled community. If we grasp that reality and that vision we shall not be afraid.

Appendix 1

Accommodation for Young People in Westminster

A report by the Revd Kenneth Leech to the meeting of the Westminster Christian Council 22 April 1968.

The world described in this paper could be termed a 'twilight zone', but it is not the twilight zone of the urban sociologists, a district of the city which, while it has not reached the night of slumdom, consists of decaying property, and where multi-occupation is the prevailing pattern of tenure. There are a number of such districts in London, but Soho is not one of them. Soho is a twilight zone of a different kind: a non-residential marginal world, in which it is people, not property, who are in the twilight, where the decay is not in houses so much as in human lives.

The existence of such a sub-world beneath the surface of the city must present problems to Westminster as a whole. But the Christian community ought to be peculiarly sensitive to the distintegration and desperation which characterises so much in the Soho scene. The institutional church, it need hardly be said, plays no role in this situation except the negative one of appearing as a bulwark of the established order and the status quo. The challenge of the young drifter is in fact a challenge to the Christian community to reconsider its own condition and function.

It was not surprising that the Social Responsibility Working Party set up by the Westminster Christian Council in 1967 reported that the most pressing need in this field within the City was that for accommodation for the large numbers of young people who were drifting about. The Working Party itself included people with experience of the needs of the beatnik groups in Trafalgar Square as well as of the varying sub-cultural strata within Soho. It was felt that in a large number of cases the possibilities for helping young people were frustrated by the lack of accommodation of an emergency type. This was particularly true of those on the 'drug fringe', the habitués of the coffee clubs, whose crises often occurred in the early hours of the morning and called for prompt action.

The discussions carried on in the Working Party were paralleled by and closely linked with other discussions elsewhere. The London Centre, a committee set up to consider the problems of missing persons in London, had recently acquired property in Notting Hill where girls could be accommodated. The Church Army had decided to develop a disused public house in Marylebone into an emergency sleeping centre, and discussions had taken place with the Westminster Council of Social Service about the possibilities of running a club there also. Other groups have been looking for property: the Association for the Prevention of Addiction, with temporary headquarters in St Anne's House, Soho, has been searching for a large house to use for homeless heroin addicts. Recently a meeting was called by the Medical Officer of Health for the City of Westminster to discuss the accommodation needs of addicts within the City.

Other groups and individuals have been active in the general field of preventative help for young people at risk. The Blenheim Project, based in Notting Hill, has been particularly concerned with the young drifters from others parts of the country. Its 1966 Report *Detached Social Work with Young Drifters in London* showed that the largest single group of young people contacted (27 per cent) came from the home counties, while the second largest was from the north-west (19 per cent). 78 per cent were homeless, and 69 per cent had used drugs (28 per cent of these being amphetamines). The National Association of Youth Clubs has developed a scheme called 'The Weekenders' which aims to contact and help the weekend adolescent population in Central London. In Soho itself, the Soho Project has its detached youth worker operating within the commercial clubs.

It is vital then that the involvement of the Westminster Christian Council should not be seen in isolation but as part of a general movement. The movement is, however, a slow one, and it is suggested that the Christian community might well act as a pressure group to impress upon the local authority and the public the urgency of the situation.

How urgent, in fact, is the need? Reliable estimates of 'homeless' persons in the Inner London area at any given time are notoriously difficult to obtain. But many of the young persons who are at risk in Westminster are not, in the strict sense, homeless: that is, they have homes and families elsewhere, and may be in frequent, if irregular, contact with them. Their relationship to the Westminster scene may involve a number of features. The largest group of all is that known as the 'weekenders', those who invade Soho on Friday and/or Saturday nights. Many of these are fundamentally stable, and come to no great harm. Included in this group, however, will be a significant delinquent section, perhaps the more disturbed elements from other London boroughs. Soho figures in their lives at weekends only (or mainly) and any help given to them must be during this time.

But alongside the weekender population, one can distinguish the 'hard core' of very disturbed youngsters who belong, if they belong anywhere, only to the marginal world of Soho. This 'hard core' includes many different social and cultural groups. The clientele of the galaxy of coffee clubs often differ markedly from each other. The homosexual clubs, the dive bars and public bars of certain pubs, the folk cellars, the clubs loosely identified with the 'underground' and the psychedelic contraculture – all these contain individuals who can be said to 'belong' only to these twilight communities.

In addition to these adolescent structures, the Trafalgar Square/ Soho complex has for some years contained members of a somewhat older group of beatniks, some of them belonging to the drug scene. These 'beat junkies' represent a very different tradition from that to which most of the newer addicts belong.

It is obvious that the provision of emergency accommodation plays only a small part in the solution of the many problems which adolescents face in Soho. Nevertheless it is a vital prerequisite at the levels both of prevention and of rehabilitation. A certain amount of rehabilitative work, for instance, of those damaged by amphetamine misuse in the clubs can only be carried on within Soho itself, within the area of infection. What is needed is a number of 'halfway houses', non-institutional hostels, where the rootless and the disturbed members of the adolescent population can receive practical help and support.

What facilities exist already, within Westminster and further afield, for helping young people in this position? The National Association of Voluntary Hostels has its headquarters in Covent Garden and acts as a clearing house for hostel accommodation of all kinds. Its officials admit that they experience extreme difficulties in placing disturbed young people, difficulties which may become almost insuperable when those concerned are dependent on drugs.

The young people themselves are unwilling to go to the more conventional hostels. (Salvation Army, Church Army, Rowton Houses, etc): many of them have already been over-institutionalised in remand centres, borstals and prisons. Hostels, for their part, are often unwilling to accept drug takers. The Bridgehead Housing Association (part of the Church of England Council for Social Aid) is responsible for implementing Home Office plans for the establishment of hostels for homeless offenders. The first of these hostels, which will take young men with drug problems, is St John's House, Deptford. But these hostels are for long-stay residence, and admission is through the recommendation of a probation officer.

What then can be offered to the young homeless boy or girl who appears in Soho late at night? The London Emergency Office at Great Guildford Street, SE1 will take young men at any hour of the night. In the same building is Southwark Reception Centre for Women, which has a remarkably homely and warm atmosphere. Camberwell Reception Centre, Consort Road, SE15, contains a large proportion of older destitute men, and seems unsuitable for young persons. Again, the image of the 'reception centre' is such that many people would sleep rough rather than go to one. There is little else that one can offer for men. In Lambeth, the Christian Action Shelter for Homeless Women at 12 Lambeth High Street, SE1, can accommodate sixteen women at short notice.

Within Soho, there are scarcely any facilities at all. The House of St Barnabas, 1 Greek Street, can take in the odd girl who is in difficulties, but beyond this there is nothing where the need is greatest. One therefore falls back constantly on individuals. Voluntary workers in the field of drug abuse in Soho, the Soho Drugs Group, have compiled lists of individuals and families who can help in emergency accommodation problems, but the beds available are almost always full; the new out-patient treatment centres for addicts are in regular contact with them about accommodation needs for patients. Charing Cross Hospital, in particular, has stressed the need for links with the local community.

It is against this background that the Church Army plan to open the Walmer Castle in Seymour Place as an emergency sleeping centre with a club attached is so important. The project should be initiated in the autumn of 1968, and a warden has been appointed. It is hoped that the Westminster Christian Council, through its member churches, will help in developing it. The Walmer Castle is almost exactly central to the City of Westminster, and therefore in a strategic position for its new role.

The following conclusions are important:

1. The Westminster Christian Council, representing the visible Christian body in the City, should act as a pressure group to stress the urgency of the need for help in the ways outlined above.

2. The Council could help the immediate crisis by encouraging those members of its congregations who are able to do so to be ready to take in young people in emergencies for short periods. This would be an expression of 'mutual responsibility' rather more relevant than the usual platitidues and vague sentiments.

3. It would be of additional value if several Council members were willing to compile lists of suitable rented accommodation within the City where young people who were trying to get back on their feet could live. A list of this kind would be invaluable to social workers, probation officers, clergy, etc.

4. The Council could perform a most valuable function by offering its services to the new out-patient treatment centre for heroin addicts at Charing Cross Hospital, 1A Bedfordbury, London WC2. It has already been suggested that people with cars available during the day could help in escorting patients to and from the centre, and there are doubtless other ways of helping which will arise.

5. The Council should offer its financial and practical help to the Church Army in the development of the Walmer Castle project. Full estimates of costs are being prepared by the Church Army, and as soon as they are available they will be reported to the Council.

As far as I am aware, no action was taken as a result of this report, none of the suggestions were taken up, and nothing came of the Working Party's work.

Appendix 2

Amphetamine Misuse

Evidence by the Revd Kenneth Leech to the
Advisory Committee on Drug Dependence, May 1969.

Amphetamine is a psychomotor stimulant. Dexamphetamine is approximately twice as potent as amphetamine. Both cause a lessening of fatigue, an increase in mental activity, and a feeling of well-being. In high doses, these substances cause a rise in blood pressure and relax the muscle of the gastric tract. Associated with these will be dryness of mouth, restlessness, headache, irritability and tremor. Very high dosage will probably also show mental depression, increased blood pressure, and some degree of disorientation, hallucinations, and convulsions. Relationships between amphetamine misuse and paranoid psychoses were suggested by Young and Scoville in 1938 and the literature on this was discussed by Connell in 1958.

Amphetamine was first synthesised by Edeleano in Germany in 1887 and further research was carried out in 1927 by Alles. Methylamphetamine was synthesised in 1919 in Japan but did not come into clinical use until 1938 in Germany. Amphetamine was first used in the treatment of depression in 1936 by Peoples and Guttman in England and by Myerson in the United States.

The conditions for which amphetamine has been prescribed include neurotic illnesses, obesity and weight control, menstrual disorders, enuresis and other behavioural disturbances in children, narcolepsy, parkinsonism, geriatrics and some terminal illnesses. It is now generally agreed that 'only in narcolepsy are amphetamines irreplaceable'. It appears that 'there are no really convincing pharmacological reasons for using a "stimulant" drug for enuresis' and it is possible that fenfluramine (Ponderax) could be as effective as an appetite suppressant. The use of other psychotropic drugs seems more effective than amphetamines in anti-depressive therapy. 'A

154

few clinical trials have demonstrated their effectiveness in mild depression, but the drugs are seldom used now'. Methylamphetamine has been used in anaesthesia and for abreaction in psychiatric practice.

'The origins of amphetamine abuse in Great Britain are not clearly documented.' By 1963 the weekend use of Dexedrine and Drinamyl (Smith, Kline and French Ltd) was established and common among adolescents in Soho. It seems probable that the misuse of Drinamyl had begun several years earlier. In Soho, both the products in misuse and the geographical centres of their circulation have remained very conservative. Information observation, including interveiws with 'pushers' and club owners, confirms that the peak period of the epidemic occurred in 1963. But Drinamyl was certainly in common use in the Soho 'pill scene' and in parts of East London among prostitutes and young delinquents a considerable time before 1963. During the period 1964–66 certain clubs were well known as sources of supply, and adolescents in Inner London boroughs were often acquainted with the names both of clubs and of individuals.

So far as the illicit market in amphetamine drugs is concerned, the proprietary products involved have principally been:

Dexedrine (Smith, Kline and French Ltd) in both tablet and spansule form.
Drinamyl (Smith, Kline and French Ltd) in tablet form chiefly.
Durophet (Riker) 12. 5 and 20 mgm capsules, and Durophet-M.
Preludin (Boehringer Ingelheim Ltd), 25 mgm tablet chiefly.
Methylamphetamine, usually in the form of Methedrine (Burroughs Wellcome Ltd) ampoules and tablets.

The young people who use the Soho coffee clubs have used Drinamyl as a 'wakeamine'. They are 'night people' who function from 9 p.m. until 9 a.m., but in many cases they are around the West End scene throughout the day also. They use amphetamines in order to survive. This applies to a lesser extent to the 'weekenders' who descend on Soho on Fridays and/or Saturdays. Their first introduction to 'blues' is invariably as a drug to keep them awake. A certain percentage of the young people who form the 'hard core' of the club structures are very disturbed, exhibit complex problems of sexual adjustment, and their amphetamine misuse is often a result of, and a symptom of, underlying disturbances. Many of these young people have had homosexual difficulties, and many have been through the (former) 'New House' of Feltham Borstal, and through Holloway Prison.

Certain external features aided the growth of the 'pillhead scene' in Soho.

1. Around Berwick Street and D'Arblay Street are, or have been, a heavily concentrated group of coffee clubs and coffee bars, at times up to eight within (literally) a stone's throw of each other. The pill traffic was easy. It is equally easy to construct a fairly accurate map of the geographical dimensions of the traffic in Soho: a heavily localised block consisting of D'Arblay Street, Wardour Mews and Berwick Street, and smaller concentration points in St Anne's Court, Gerrard Street, part of Charing Cross Road, and Coventry Street. Up to 1966 Great Windmill Street, and up to 1967 Oxford Street, would have been included.

2. Between 1966 and 1968 the major source of supply of injectible methylamphetamine as well as of oral amphetamines was the surgeries of two well-known doctors. One of these is now in prison, and the other has been removed from the medical register. The methylamphetamine epidemic, which reached its peak in 1968, was the most important single element in the recent growth of the Soho drug subculture. Some of its features have recently been studied. I have myself described the phenomenon elsewhere thus:

> The spread of injectible methylamphetamine usually in the form of Methedrine (Burroughs Wellcome 30 mgm) ampoules during 1966–68 was the biggest single epidemiological problem in Soho. The spread of methylamphetamine misuse can be mapped with the most frightening accuracy, and it was this spread which brought the 'pep pill fringe' and the hard drug subculture closer together. It is our belief that historically, in Soho at any rate, the 'escalation' role often attributed to cannabis has in fact been played by methylamphetamine, the use of which created a body of quasi-addicts and introduced the ritual of injection into the pill scene.

It is difficult to estimate the age and sex distribution of amphetamine users. In the West End perhaps some 60 per cent of regular users are male. The average age of both male and female users in this area is probably 18–19. Children under 16 are rarely seen in the Soho club structures, but there are very large numbers aged 17 and over. Amphetamines are seen as part of the 'furniture' of the Soho scene. Because of Soho's role as an infection and distribution point, the numbers of young people in other areas who are affected must run into many thousands.

The most significant patterns of 'progression' which can be traced are as follows.

1. *from oral amphetamine to injectible amphetamine*
   After the restrictions on injectible methylamphetamine in October 1968 there was a minor epidemic of methylphenidate (Ritalin, Ciba Laboratories Ltd) misuse. Since the end of 1968 there has been a marked increase in the crushing and injecting of Dexedrine and, to a lesser extent, of Drinamyl, although the latter is not popular as an injection as it is regarded as being too hard to crush.

2. *from oral amphetamine to injection of other substances*
   Intravenous use of barbiturates and other hypnotics has increased but most of those involved are heroin and methadone (Physeptone) users who supplement as well as potentiate their heroin in this way. But some non-opiate users have been known to 'fix' Tuinal, Nembutal, Desbutal (which contains methylamphetamine) and methaqualone (Mandrax).

3. *from amphetamines to Physeptone*
   This has been most marked. The spread of Physeptone among former 'pillheads' has increased enormously.

The spread of intravenous methylamphetamine use in the West End acted as a link between three loosely structured groups of young people: the junkies of the 'Dilly'; the beats and drifters of Trafalgar Square and Covent Garden; and the pillheads of the Soho clubs. Historically the introduction of injectible methylamphetamine into the drug scene on a significant scale was through its substitution for cocaine by two general practitioners prescribing for addicts. But it spread rapidly among the young drifters. A report by one project working with drifters in West London noted in 1966:

An interesting sub-group were those who used Methedrine only. Although an amphetamine, this drug is taken intravenously and its users tend to conform to the pattern of behaviour common to heroin users. Methedrine users tend to accept the beatnik philosophy, taking some security from the fact that their drug was an amphetamine but enjoying their participation in the overt ritual of those they considered to be 'real' addicts.

Another group reported in 1968:

> One reason at least why Methedrine is so popular amongst our young people is that it has two side effects which are positive 'props' to their particular way of life. (i) It enables them to stay awake for long hours, often necessary when living rough, and (ii) it reduces considerably their immediate need for food. In addition there are such vast amounts available on the black market (due largely to over-prescription) that it can be bought at a very cheap price anywhere in the West End.

Recently the managers of three all-night coffee clubs in Soho were asked, during one evening, about their knowledge of sources of supply of amphetamines. All of them mentioned one particular doctor in Soho as a major source. Two of them, independently, mentioned Welwyn Garden City, but did not know the name of any factory there. Altogether, four doctors were mentioned as sources of significant supplies, one in Soho, one in north-west London, and two in the Notting Hill and Paddington areas. Other Soho club members were contemptuous of any claims that security measures at Smith, Kline and French's factory were adequate, though none offered reliable evidence of significant leakages. It has been claimed that 'at least 80 per cent of the Drinamyl sold illegally in Soho ... has been stolen during the manufacturing process by employees of the manufacturing firm' but again there seems to be no evidence in support of this claim.

It seems likely that the habit of crushing and injecting amphetamines will continue, and, whatever the source, there is no shortage of pills in Soho. There is a very urgent need for out-patient clinics to which amphetamine users can be referred, and there is a need for one such clinic in Soho itself. Since the root problems of these young people are usually emotional, psychosexual, perhaps spiritual ones, there would seem to be a need for more clinics on Tavistock Centre lines. Prevention of all drug experimentation is impossible and perhaps undesirable. What is needed in instruction on the wider field of the use of chemicals in medicine and science, and 'drug problems' should only be 'taught' against this background. Any attempt to isolate drug misuse as a separate 'problem' either in education or in therapy should be resisted.

Appendix 3

A Sermon

*Preached at Canterbury Cathedral by the Revd Kenneth Leech on
7 July 1973 at a Solemn Mass organised by the Catholic societies of
the diocese.*

You cannot serve God and Mammon. Matt. 6:24.

It is exactly fifty years since the Anglo-Catholic Congress of 1923
at which Bishop Frank Weston delivered his memorable address.
His words are even more relevant today than they were at the time.

I say to you, and I say it to you with all the earnestness that I
have, that if you are prepared to fight for the right of adoring
Jesus in the Blessed Sacrament, then you have got to come out
from behind your tabernacle, and walk, with Christ mystically
present in you, out into the streets of this country, and find the
same Jesus in the people of your cities and your villages. You
cannot claim to worship Jesus in the tabernacle if you do not
pity Jesus in the slum.

Now mark this – this is gospel truth. If you are prepared to
say that the Anglo-Catholic is at perfect liberty to rake in all the
money he can get, no matter what the wages are that are paid,
no matter what the conditions are under which people work; if
you say that the Anglo-Catholic has a right to hold his peace
while his fellow-citizens are living in hovels below the level of the
streets, this I say to you, that you do not yet know the Lord Jesus
in his sacrament. . .

It is folly – it is madness – to suppose that you can worship
Jesus in the sacrament and Jesus on the throne of glory when
you are sweating him in the souls and bodies of his children. It
cannot be done. . .

These words were typical of many uttered from the Anglo-Catholic
pulpits of this period. Listen again, for this is also the sixtieth

159

anniversary of the Church Socialist League's conference of 1913 when Canon Percy Widdrington said these words:

> The church has been too long the Church Quiescent here on earth, content to serve as the scavenger of the capitalist system. If it refuses the challenge it may survive as a pietistic sect providing devotional opportunities for a small and dwindling section of the community, a residuary solace for the world's defeated, administering religion as an anaesthetic to help men to endure the hateful operation of life, an ambulance picking up the wounded, entered on the Charities Register – an institution among institutions. But it will cease to be the organ of the Kingdom, building up the world out of itself: it will have abandoned its mission and become apostate.

One could quote much more from the same period. At the 1920 Congress Father Thornton was saying that the greatest need was to rediscover the vision of the Kingdom of God on earth, and Canon Widdrington, in a volume which appeared a few years later, was claiming that such a rediscovery of the good news of the Kingdom would bring about a new reformation compared with which the Reformation of the sixteenth century would appear trivial. Earlier Father Adderley was saying that the Mass was the weekly meeting of rebels against a Mammon worshipping world order. 'You cannot serve God and Mammon' was understood in those days. They were the days of Dolling in Portsmouth, and of Stanton at St Alban's, Holborn. These men must be turning in their graves today.

What these early Anglo-Catholics possessed, and what we most manifestly do not possess, was a theology and a social conscience, and the two were inseparable. The conflict between God and Mammon grew out of their theology, for they were men whose lives and thought were rooted in the incarnation and the sacraments. Today we are part of a church which serves God weakly and Mammon strongly. But on the 50th anniversary of Bishop Weston's speech, on the 60th anniversary of Widdrington's, and on the 140th anniversary of the beginning of the Oxford Movement, where is the Anglo-Catholic movement now? It is a movement which has clearly lost its way, and which is obsessed with trivia. So, confronted with international racism and oppression, with war and injustice, with a situation where some two hundred multinational firms will soon control the bulk of the world's economy, we are discussing Series 3 and the ordination of women. I sometimes think that when the nuclear bombs have exploded and the world is devastated, some-where on an island in the South Pacific the brave Anglo-Catholic remnant will sit amid radio-active dust discussing valid orders. We are more concerned with changes in the liturgy than with changes in the world. Ritual change has taken the place of social change. We would do well (if I may be spared another quote) to take to heart the words of another famous priest, Father Charles Marson, when he appeared before the ridiculous Royal Commission on Ecclesiastical Discipline in 1905, to answer charges of ritual atroci-ties, such as wearing vestments and bowing. After his evidence, Marson said:

> If the Commissioners wish for any further information as to our clothes, chandlery, or as to which of our joints we crook in worship, I shall be delighted to give them every information. But I beg leave to point out that the lives of Christ's poor are starved and stunted, that their wages are low, their houses often bad and insanitary, and their minds full of darkness and despair. These are the real disorders of the church.

At the risk of being dubbed an obscurantist I believe that we can learn more from these pioneer priests of the movement than we have done.

For if there is to be a Catholic revival in the Church of England, it will centre upon the recovery of authentic Catholic social proph-ecy and of authentic Catholic spirituality. The prophetic voice and the spirit of inner prayer are not two alternative ways of Christian witness: they are inseparable in a healthy Christian life, and history shows that where they are not held together, both decay. First, we need to rediscover the vision of the Kingdom of God and of the hope of the transformation of the earth. The real division among the Christians of the future is going to be about this vision: it will be the division between those who believe that the gospel has a hope for this world and for human society, and those who do not. Many who call themselves Catholic in this respect are only Catholic in externals: at heart, in their assumptions and their thought, they are protestant individualists. They have accepted the basic heresy that Christianity is only concerned with saving individual souls, and they have accepted the doctrine of the two kingdoms which are quite separate. This is not Catholicism. Catholicism is concerned with the redemption of the whole world, and it is this total vision which we need to recover. The early Catholic rebels realised that the clash between God and Mammon followed inevitably from their theology; that if they took seriously the doctrines of the incarnation, of the Kingdom, and of the Mass, this had revolutionary social and political consequences.

Secondly, there will only be a Catholic revival if there is a recovery of inner spirituality. In the last few years I have been in close touch with very large numbers of young people who have turned for spiritual guidance to eastern gurus, for spiritual guidance they assumed western Christianity was too superficial to provide. And this revival of the spiritual quest was occurring throughout the so-called 'trendy sixties', that decade when the church was at its most 'relevant' and activist, when deans were jumping in parachutes, when young curates were rushing about feverishly trying to be 'with it', and when many priests seemed to spend all their time doing every other job except their own. While all this was happening, many of the young were turning elsewhere for their spiritual strength: to Maharishi, Hare Krishna, Guru Maharaj Ji. The most desperate need at present among priests is not for more socially active clergy, for more 'involved' clergy, and so on (although these things are important), but for more priests who are competent spiritual directors, for priests whose lives are steeped in prayer and contemplation.

We are on the verge of a spiritual revolution in the west. But the direction it will take is by no means clear. In many ways the similiarities with the early Christian centuries are close. There were two great enemies of the early church: gnosticism, the false spirituality which divided the world from the 'spirit', and the totalitarian state, nicknamed in the Book of Revelation as 'Babylon the great, the mother of prostitutes'. Today we see a new gnosticism, esoteric spiritualities of all kinds, astrology, spiritualism, occult magic, and we see concentrated power and wealth, and a church which has long ago accepted and acquiesced in an unjust order. If there is to be Catholic revival, we must recover a true spirituality and we must recover a prophetic voice, and the two are inseparable. As Daniel Berrigan says, the time will soon be upon us when the pursuit of contemplation will be a strictly subversive activity. A praying church will soon become a prophetic church, a dangerous church.

We need nothing so much as a new Anglo-Catholic revival, a new Oxford Movement. But we need not wait for it to come from Oxford, and it will not come from there. It could begin now, and it could begin here.

References

Chapter 1: On the Edge

1. Henry Mayhew, *London Labour and the London Poor*, Griffin, Bohn and Co. 1861; John Hollingshead, *Ragged London in 1861*, Smith Elder and Co. 1861; Charles Booth, *Life and Labour of the People in London*, Macmillan 17 vols, 1902–3. For the notion of 'outcast London' see Gareth Stedman Jones, *Outcast London*, Oxford, Clarendon Press 1971.
2. Charles Dickens, 'Health by Act of Parliament', *Household Words* 1, 1850, p. 463.
3. See *The Communist Manifesto*; K. Marx, *The 18th Brumaire of Louis Bonaparte*; F. Engels, preface to *The Peasants' War in Germany*, etc. See also E. J. Hobsbawm, *Bandits*, Penguin 1972, and Stuart Hall *et al. Policing the Crisis*, Hutchinson 1978.
4. A. M. Field *et al. 1971 Census Data on London Overseas Born Population and their Children*, GLC Intelligence Unit 1974.
5. See David Smith, *North and South: Britain's economic, social and political divide*, Penguin 1989; Doreen Massey, 'Heartlands of defeat', *Marxism Today*, July 1987, pp. 18–23, and 'A new class of geography', ibid., May 1988, pp. 12–17.
6. *Faith in the City: a call to action by church and nation*, Church House Publishing 1985; David Sheppard, 'The poverty that imprisons the spirit', Dimbleby Lecture 1984, *The Listener*, 19 April 1984, pp. 8–12; and *Bias to the Poor*, Hodder and Stoughton 1983.
7. See C. A. R. Crosland, *The Future of Socialism*, Cape 1956; Douglas Jay, *Socialism and the New Society*, Longmans 1962; Ferdinand Zweig, *The Worker in an Affluent Society*, Heinemann 1961. See also John Westergaard, 'Sociology: the myth of classless-

ness' in Robin Blackburn ed., *Ideology in Social Science*, Fontana 1977, pp. 119–63.

8. See Ruth Glass, *Newcomers: the West Indians in London*, Centre for Urban Studies 1960, pp. 133–4; *London: Aspects of Change*, Centre for Urban Studies 1964; Ruth Glass and John Westergaard, *London's Housing Needs*, Centre for Urban Studies 1965, p. 44. The key essays are contained in Ruth Glass, *Cliches of Urban Doom and other essays*, Blackwell 1988. There are references to gentrification in Notting Hill in the Centre for Urban Studies' Quinquennial Report 1958–62, pp. 23–7. My debt to the late Ruth Glass for her insight, friendship and inspiration over many years is incalculable. She died as this book was going to press.

9. Robert Park, 'Human migration and the marginal man', *American Journal of Sociology* 33, 1928, pp. 181–3. See also Gino Germani, *Marginality*, New Brunswick, NJ, Transaction Books 1980.

10. On the life of Cable Street see Michael Banton, *The Coloured Quarter*, Cape 1955. See also Kenneth Leech, 'Goodbye to Cable Street', *Institute of Race Relations Newsletter*, January 1964, pp. 5–6; 'The East London drug traffic', *Social Work* 24: 2, April 1966, pp. 23–7; and 'Human casualties in a crisis district', *East London Papers* 11: 1, Summer 1968, pp. 3–19.

11. Ashley Smith, *The East Enders*, Secker and Warburg 1961, p. 75.

12. George Foulser, 'Cablestrasse', *The Observer*, 28 August 1960.

13. Banton, op. cit., p. 28.

14. Roi Ottley, *No Green Pastures*, John Murray 1952, p. 29.

15. Vivien Batchelor, *John Bull*, 6 December 1947.

16. *Daily Mail*, 31 October 1947.

17. *Regula non-bullata*, ch. 9. See Leonardo Boff, *St Francis: a model for human liberation*, SCM Press 1985.

18. On Father Neville see Kenneth Leech, *Spirituality and Pastoral Care*, Sheldon Press 1986, pp. 85–94.

19. See Joseph Williamson, *Father Joe*, Hodder and Stoughton 1963. See also Kenneth Leech, Dolling Lecture 1989 'The End of the Dolling Era? Father Joe Williamson in Stepney', to be published in 1990 by the Jubilee Group, St Clement's House, Sirdar Road, London W11.

20. On Stanley Evans see Kenneth Leech, *Spirituality and Pastoral Care*, op. cit. pp. 95–104.

21. See W. D. Miller, *A Harsh and Dreadful Love*, New York, Livre-

wright 1973, and *Dorothy Day: a biography*, Harper and Row 1982; Mel Piehl, *Breaking Bread: the Catholic Worker and the origins of Catholic radicalism in America*, Philadelphia, Temple University Press 1982. *The Catholic Worker* is still published monthly.

22. Kenneth Leech, 'The church and the social outcast', *Prism* 81, June 1964, pp. 9–14.

23. Booth, op. cit., 2nd Series, vol. 2, p. 111: 'Hoxton is the leading criminal quarter of London and indeed of all England. Wall off Hoxton, it is said, and nine-tenths of the criminals of London would be walled off.'

24. See *The Institute of Charity (The Rosminian Fathers) 1835–1985*, p. 4; Kit Cunningham, letter in *The Independent*, 27 May 1989.

25. See Derek Cox, *A Community Approach to Youth Work in East London*, YWCA 1970.

26. David Downes, *The Delinquent Solution*, Routledge 1966.

27. Mary Morse, *The Unattached*, Penguin 1965; G. W. Goetschius and M. J. Tasch, *Working with Unattached Youth*, Routledge 1967.

28. See Geof Bevan, 'The Skinhead in Notting Hill', MS, St Anne's House, Soho, 1970; *Soho Project Report* 1972; Michael Farrant and Howard Marchant, *Making Contact with Unattached Youth*, Manchester Youth Development Trust, March 1971.

29. *Manchester City Centre Project Report*, October 1972.

30. Peter Burton, 'Girls on the gay scene', *Jeremy* 1: 7, 1970, pp. 17–20; and 'Homosexuality in the West End', MS, St Anne's House, Soho, 3 November 1970.

31. John Fortunato, *AIDS: the spiritual dilemma*, Harper and Row 1987, p. 11.

32. Rowan Wiliams in *Speaking Love's Name: homosexuality: some catholic and socialist reflections*, ed. Ashley Beck and Ros Hunt, Jubilee Group 1988, p. 1.

33. *Report of the Committee of Inquiry into Homelessness*, London County Council, Agenda Paper 4171, 17 July 1962.

34. Sally Trench, *Bury Me in My Boots*, Hodder and Stoughton 1968.

35. *The Rink Report 1968–69*, Appendix 1, Social Survey by G. A. Batten, Rink Project 1970.

36. J. H. Briscoe-Smith, letter, 20 March 1968.

37. *The Observer*, 6 November 1988.

38. *Centrepoint Annual Report*, 1971.

39. ibid. See also the report for 1972–3.

40. Ron Bailey, *Shelter Report on Bed and Breakfast*, Shelter 1974;

Hotels for Homeless Families?, Shelter Westminster Action Team 1974; *The Times*, 8 August 1978; *The Observer*, 6 November 1988.

41. Brendan O'Mahony, *A Capital Offence: the plight of the young single homeless in London*, Routledge and Barnardos 1988, p. 20.

42. John Greve, *Investigation into Homelessness in London, Interim Report*, University of Leeds, October 1985.

43. *The Guardian*, 27 March 1986. See also 42 above.

44. *The Guardian*, 10 October 1989.

45. *The Independent*, 5 March 1987.

46. *The Observer*, 6 November 1988.

47. Geoffrey Randall, *Homeless and Hungry: a sign of the times*, Centrepoint 1989.

48. Cited in *In and Against the State*, Pluto Press 1980, p. 44.

49. On the 'Dilly boys' see Jane Alexander, 'The Circus', *New Society*, 15 May 1969; Mervyn Harris, 'The Dilly Boys', *New Society*, 6 April 1972, pp. 6–8, and *The Dilly Boys*, 1973; Andrew Tyler, 'Piccadilly rent boy', *New Society*, 22–29 December 1983, pp. 483–5; Tim Hughes, 'Piccadilly report', *Jeremy* 1:23, 1969, pp. 22–5; Kate Muir, 'Streetwise and money poor', *The Independent*, 4 January 1989.

50. David Randall, unpublished MS. For a version of this MS see his contribution to *Embracing the Chaos*, ed. James Woodward, SPCK 1990.

51. John Fortunato, op. cit., p. 35.

52. L. William Countryman, 'The AIDS crisis: theological and ethical reflections', *Anglican Theological Review* 69: 2, April 1987, pp. 125–34.

53. Alastair V. Campbell, *Rediscovering Pastoral Care*, Darton, Longman and Todd 1981, p. 37.

54. Simon Watney, 'The wrong ideas that are plaguing AIDS', *The Guardian*, 16 October 1987.

55. Kosuke Koyama, 'Towards a crucified mind', *Waterbuffalo Theology*, SCM Press 1974, pp. 209–24.

56. Carl E. Wennerstrom in J. Luther Adams and Seward Hiltner eds, *Pastoral Care in the Liberal Churches*, Nashville, Abingdon Press 1970, pp. 37–8.

57. On the ministry of Jesus see Richard J. Cassidy, *Jesus, Politics and Society: a study in Luke's Gospel*, Maryknoll, Orbis Press 1978; Walter Pilgrim, *Rich and Poor in Luke's Gospel*, Minneapolis, Augsburg Press 1981; James A. Sanders, 'The ethic of election in Luke's Great Banquet parable' in J. L. Crenshaw and J. T.

Willis eds, *Essays in Old Testament Ethics*, New York, Ktav 1974, pp. 247–71.

58. Rowan Williams, *Resurrection*, Darton, Longman and Todd 1987, pp. 12, 16.

59. David Jenkins, *The Contradiction of Christianity*, SCM Press 1976, p. 49.

60. *Catholic Social Teaching and the US Economy*, 1984, para. 54. See further Donal Dorr, *Option for the Poor: a hundred years of Vatican social teaching*, Maryknoll, Orbis 1983.

61. Karl Barth, *Der Romerbrief*, 1st edn Bern 1919, p. 366.

62. R. H. Tawney, *Religion and the Rise of Capitalism*, 1926, p. 268.

63. Thomas Merton, *Raids on the Unspeakable*, Burns and Oates 1977, pp. 51–2.

64. Thomas Merton, *The Climate of Monastic Prayer*, Spencer, Mass, Cistercian Publications 1969, p. 35.

65. Dietrich Bonhoeffer, *Letters and Papers from Prison*, New York, Macmillan 1972, p. 17.

Chapter 2: Opium of the People

1. For a more detailed account of the counter-culture see Kenneth Leech, *Youthquake: the growth of a counter-culture through two decades*, Sheldon Press 1973.

2. Such a simplistic dismissal of a decade seems to be an integral part of the rhetoric of the new right both here and in the USA. Examples of such rhetoric are so numerous that only a few must suffice here. Margaret Thatcher has spoken of our society 'reaping what was sown in the 60s' with its 'fashionable theories and permissive claptrap'. Norman Tebbit has blamed the rise of social violence on 'the end of National Service and the emergence of flower power'. Similar accounts can be found in articles and speeches over the years by Peregrine Worsthorne, Mary Whitehouse, Colin Welch, Edward Norman, and many others. For a useful corrective to such accounts see David Edgar, 'Never too old: learning from the 60s', *New Socialist*, May 1986, pp. 18–20.

3. See *Rector's Notebook*, All Saints Church, Haight-Ashbury, 28 March 1967, and 20 January 1970.

4. Episcopal Diocese of California, San Francisco Deanery, statement of 13 June 1967.

5. The statement was made in a letter to *The Times*, 16 September 1967.

6. Caroline Coon, 'The hippy and the psychedelic scene', MS, St Anne's House, Soho, 4 March 1969.

7. Simon Tugwell, OP, 'Thoughts of a monknik', *New Blackfriars* 50: 593, October 1969, pp. 709–12.

8. On the wider cultural background see Kenneth Leech, *Youthquake*, op. cit. On the Haight-Ashbury drug culture see David E. Smith, John Luce and Ernest A. Dernburg, 'Love needs care: Haight-Ashbury dies', *New Society*, 16 July 1970, pp. 98–101; David E. Smith, 'Changing drug patterns in Haight-Ashbury', *California Medicine* 110, 1969, pp. 151–7; David E. Smith, 'The San Francisco drug scene', MS, St Anne's House, Soho, 17 September 1970.

9. Cited in David Caute, *Sixty-Eight: the year of the barricades*, Hamish Hamilton 1988, p. 36.

10. Robert Elms, *New Socialist*, May 1986.

11. On Petro see Kenneth Leech, 'John Petro, the junkies' doctor', *New Society*, 11 June 1981, pp. 430–2.

12. *Drug Addiction*, Second Report of the Interdepartmental Committee, HMSO 1966, paras 11 and 12.

13. See Kenneth Leech 'The junkies' doctors and the London drug scene in the 1960s: some remembered fragments' in P. T. Bean and D. K. Whynes eds, *Policing and Prescribing*, to be published by Macmillan in 1990.

14. Kenneth Leech and Brenda Jordan, *Drugs for Young People: their use and misuse*, Religious Education Press 1967.

15. Ian Pierce James, introduction to Kenneth Leech, *A Practical Guide to the Drug Scene*, SPCK 1973, p. vii.

16. Kenneth Leech, *The Drug Scene from St Anne's, Soho*, 1968, p. 1.

17. Anton Wallich-Clifford, *The Simon Scene*, Simon Community 1968, pp. 18–19. According to David Brandon, a leading expert on homelessness, the influence of the Simon Community represented 'the major philosophical impact on the residential field', see David Brandon, 'Homelessness and vagrancy in London', MS, St Anne's House, Soho, 23 February 1971.

18. Laurie Little in *The Soho Project Report*, 1969, p. 15.

19. William Burroughs, *Junkie*, New English Library 1966 edn, p. 12.

20. Kenneth Robinson, 'World in Action', Granada TV, 12 February 1968.

21. *God in a Pill? Meher Baba on LSD and the High Roads*, San Francisco, Sufism Reoriented, 1966.

22. Benjamin Paul Blood, *The Anaesthetic Revelation and the Gist of Philosophy*, 1874; William James, *The Varieties of Religious Experience*, Longmans 1902; Aldous Huxley, *Heaven and Hell*, Penguin 1956.
23. Alan Watts, *The Joyous Cosmology*, Random House 1962; Timothy Leary, Ralph Metzner and Richard Alpert, *The Psychedelic Experience*, New Jersey, University Books 1966; Timothy Leary, *The Politics of Ecstasy*, MacGibbon and Kee 1971.
24. See Kenneth Leech, *Youthquake*, op. cit., ch. 3.
25. Frank Lake, *Clinical Theology*, Darton, Longman and Todd 1966.
26. *The Psychedelic Experience*, op. cit., p. 11.
27. Theodore Roszak, *The Making of a Counter Culture*, Faber 1968, p. 177.
28. William Sargent, 'The physiology of faith', *New Society*, 17 July 1969, p. 92.
29. Allan Y. Cohen, 'LSD and the search for God', MS, St Anne's House, Soho, 1969. This paper was published by the Church Literature Association in 1974. See also Allan Y. Cohen, 'Who takes LSD and why?', *New Society*, 11 August 1966, pp. 226–8.
30. Thomas Merton, *The Sign of Jonas*, Burns and Oates 1953, p. 41.
31. Ulrich Simon, *A Theology of Auschwitz*, Gollancz 1967, p. 124.
32. Bruce Kenrick, *Come Out the Wilderness*, Fontana 1965, pp. 155, 169.

Chapter 3: Midnight Hour

1. R. D. Laing, *The Politics of Experience and The Bird of Paradise*, Penguin 1971 edn, p. 118.
2. ibid. p. 136, See also Laing's essay in *The Role of Religion in Mental Health*, National Association of Mental Health 1967.
3. John Michell, *City of Revelation*, 1972, p. 55.
4. Theodore Roszak, *Unfinished Animal*, Faber 1975, p. 68.
5. Laurie Taylor, *New Society*, 4 October 1973.
6. Thomas Merton, *Conjectures of a Guilty Bystander*, Burns and Oates 1968 edn, p. 58.
7. Cited in George Woodcock, *Thomas Merton, Monk and Poet*, Edinburgh, Canongate Press 1978, pp. 41–2.
8. Thomas Merton, *The Climate of Monastic Prayer*, Spencer, Mass, Cistercian Publications 1969, p. 35. See also *The Asian Journal of Thomas Merton*, Sheldon Press 1973, p. 333f.

9. Evagrius, *De Oratione* 60.
10. David Schuller *et al.*, *Ministry in America*, Harper and Row 1980, p. 74.
11. See Karol Wojtyla [Pope John Paul II], *Faith According to St John of the Cross*, San Francisco, Ignatius Press 1981, p. 142.
12. See ref. 7 above.
13. *The Sign of Jonas*, op. cit., pp. 266–7.
14. Gilbert Shaw, *Christian Prayer: a way of progress*, Oxford, SLG Press 1970, p. 20.
15. I have taken the phrase from the title of a talk, given in various places, by David Jenkins. A book by Jenkins on this theme is to be published soon.
16. See Alasdair MacIntyre, *After Virtue*, Duckworth 1981, and *Whose Justice? Which Rationality?*, Duckworth 1988.
17. Alasdair MacIntyre, 'A society without a metaphysics', *The Listener*, 13 September 1956, pp. 375–6.
18. Richard J. Neuhaus, *The Naked Public Square*, Grand Rapids, Eerdmans 1986 edn.
19. MacIntyre, *After Virtue*, op. cit., p. 245.
20. See Stanley Hauerwas, *Vision and Virtue*, 1974; *A Community of Character*, 1981; and *The Peaceable Kingdom*, 1983, all published by the University of Notre Dame Press.
21. See J. B. Metz, *Theology of the World*, 1965, and *Faith in History and Society*, 1980, both published by Burns and Oates.
22. Nicholas Lash, *Theology on the Way to Emmaus*, SCM Press 1986, p. 200.
23. Martin Luther King, *Strength to Love*, Fontana 1969, pp. 23–4.
24. H. A. Williams, *Becoming What I Am*, Darton, Longman and Todd 1977, p. 86f.
25. Marcel Legaut, *True Humanity*, New York, Paulist Press 1982, p. 21.
26. J. B. Chautard, *The Soul of the Apostolate*, Louisville, KY, Abbey of Gethsemani, 1946, p. 103f.
27. Segundo Galilea, 'Liberation as an encounter with politics and contemplation' in Richard Woods, OP, ed., *Understanding Mysticism*, Athlone Press 1981, pp. 529–40.
28. Marian Leighton, 'Victoria Woodhull meets Karl Marx: spirituality and the radical movement', *Liberation* [USA], Fall 1977, p. 16.
29. Sheila Rowbotham *et al.*, *Beyond the Fragments: feminism and the making of socialism*, Merlin Press 1979, p. 23.

30. ibid. pp. 118–19.
31. Alan W. Jones, *Journey into Christ*, New York, Seabury Press 1977, p. 15.
32. Thomas Merton, *Zen and the Birds of Appetite*, New York, New Directions 1968, p. 76f.
33. R. D. Laing, *The Politics of Experience and The Bird of Paradise*, Penguin 1970 edn, p. 12.
34. V. I. Lenin, *What Is To Be Done?*, cited in Rowbotham, op. cit. p. 111.
35. Gregory Nazianzen, *Theological Orations* in E. R. Hardy ed., *Christology of the Later Fathers*, Philadelphia, Westminster Press 1954, p. 136; cf. Leonardo and Clodovis Boff, *Salvation and Liberation*, Maryknoll, Orbis Press 1929, p. 2: any theology which is not based on spiritual experience is said to be no more than 'religious breathlessness'.

Chapter 4: The Mark of Cain

1. On the rise of the NF in the inner urban areas see Christopher T. Husbands, *Racial Exclusionism and the City: the urban support for the National Front*, Allen Lane 1982.
2. J. M. Winter and D. M. Joslin eds, *R. H. Tawney's Commonplace Book, Economic History Review* Supplement 5, Cambridge University Press 1972, p. 13.
3. On the sacramental socialist tradition see Donald Gray, *Earth and Altar*, Alcuin Club Collections 68, 1986; and John R. Orens, 'Priesthood and prophecy: the development of Anglo-Catholic socialism' in Kenneth Leech and Rowan Williams eds, *Essays Catholic and Radical*, Bowerdean Press 1983, pp. 158–80. The tradition is represented today in the thinking and writings of the Jubilee Group, St Clement's House, Sirdar Road, London W11.
4. 'World in Action', Granada TV, 30 January 1978.
5. *The Times*, 5 August 1967.
6. Professor Robert Moore: 'The keystone of modern racism', *Movement* 41, Summer 1980, p. 4; 'The foundation document in the history of contemporary racism', *The Guardian*, 16 April 1988. For more detailed treatment see Robert Moore and Tina Wallace, *Slamming the Door: the administration of immigration control*, Martin Robertson 1975, p. 2: 'These principles were to be the basis of all future legislation. The principles were, quite simply,

that black people were, in themselves, a problem, and that the fewer we had of them in the UK the better it would be.'

7. *Our First Eight Years: the achievements of the Conservative Government since 1979*, The Conservative Party 1987, p. 18.
8. Martin Barker, *The New Racism*, Junction Books 1981.
9. Cited in Francesa Klug and Paul Gordon, 'Boiling into fascism', *New Statesman*, 10 June 1983, pp. 12–13.
10. See Paul Gordon and David Rosenberg, *Daily Racism*, Runnymede Trust 1989.
11. J. H. Oldham, *Christianity and the Race Problem*, SCM Press 1924; William Temple in *International Review of Mission* 31: 51, July 1924.
12. *Teaching Christian Ethics*, SCM Press 1974, p. 104.
13. John Tiller, *A Strategy for the Church's Ministry*, Church Information Office 1983, pp. 11, 12–14.
14. Kenneth Cracknell, David Jennings and Christine Trethowan, *Blind Leaders for the Blind?* Birmingham, AFFOR, 1982.
15. *Learning in Diversity*, Catholic Media Office, July 1984, pp. 55, 58–60.
16. Heather Walton, *A Tree God Planted: black people in British Methodism*, Ethnic Minorities in Methodism Working Party, 1985.
17. Urban Ministry Project, 'Urban training: a plea for priority', *Christian Action Journal*, Autumn 1984, para. 1:2.
18. Leonardo Boff, *Church, Charism and Power*, SCM Press 1985, p. 54.
19. *Race and Immigration*, Runnymede Trust Bulletin, September 1985, p. 5. The Code of Practice came into operation on 1 April 1984.
20. Karl Marx, preface to *Capital*, English edn, 1867; Moscow, Foreign Languages Publishing House, 1958 edn, vol. 1, p. 10.

Chapter 5: What's in it for Whitechapel Road?

1. Cited in Maurice Reckitt, *P. E. T. Widdrington*, SPCK 1961, p. 57.
2. Address to a fringe meeting of the Synod, 10 February 1988, reported in most newspapers on the 11. See also Douglas Hurd, 'God versus Caesar?', *Church Times*, 9 September 1988, where the same points are made.
3. Maurice Reckitt, *Religion and Social Purpose*, SPCK 1935, p. 12.
4. Peter Selby, *Liberating God*, SPCK 1983, p. 88.

5. Robert Lambourne, 'Objections to a proposed national pastoral organisation', *Contact* 35, June 1971, pp. 25–7.

6. Seward Hiltner, *Pastoral Counselling*, 1949; *Preface to Pastoral Theology*, 1958; and *The Christian Shepherd*, 1959, all published by Abingdon Press, Nashville; Frank Lake, *Clinical Theology*, Darton, Longman and Todd 1966.

7. Walter Brueggeman, 'The prophet as a destablising presence' in Earl E. Shelp and Ronald H. Sunderland eds, *The Pastor as Prophet*, New York, Pilgrim Press 1985, pp. 49–77.

8. *Faith in the City*, op. cit., p. 55.

9. Stanley Hauerwas, *Vision and Virtue*, op. cit., p. 7.

10. Alasdair MacIntyre, *Whose Justice? Which Rationality?* op. cit., p. x.

11. Dorothee Soelle in *Concilium* 143, T. & T. Clark 1981, p. 70.

12. Edward Farley, *Theologia: the fragmentation and unity of theological education*, Philadelphia, Fortress Press 1983; and 'Theology and practice outside the clerical paradigm' in Don S. Browning ed., *Practical Theology*, Harper and Row 1983, pp. 21–41.

13. David Tracy, *The Analogical Imagination*, New York, Crossroad 1981, ch. 1, 'A social portrait of the theologian', pp. 3–46.

14. B. J. F. Lonergan, *Method in Theology*, Darton, Longman and Todd 1972, pp. 326–7.

15. From a paper by Bernice Martin. I have not been able to trace the exact reference.

16. Kenneth Cracknell and Christopher Lamb, *Theology on Full Alert*, British Council of Churches 1984, p. 4.

17. Laurie Green, *Power to the Powerless*, Marshall Pickering 1987, p. 10.

18. Evagrius, *De Oratione* 60.

19. A. M. Allchin ed., *Theology and Prayer*, Fellowship of St Alban and St Sergius 1975; George Dragas, *The Meaning of Theology: an essay in Greek patristics*, Darlington 1980; Frank Whaling, 'The development of the word "theology" ', *Scottish Journal of Theology* 34: 4, 1981, pp. 289–312; Steven Peter Tsichlis, 'The nature of theology in the *Theological Orations* of St Gregory Nazianzen', *Diakonia* 16: 3, 1981, pp. 238–46.

20. *Church Times*, 25 September 1987.

21. Antonio Gramsci, *Selections from the Prison Notebooks*, Lawrence and Wishart 1971. See Anne Showstack Sassoon, *Gramsci's Politics*, Hutchinson 1987, pp. 134–50 on the role of intellectuals.

22. Sharon Welch, *Communities of Resistance and Solidarity*, Maryknoll, Orbis Press 1985, p. 74.

23. Andrew Kirk, *Theology Encounters Revolution*, 1980; and *Theology and the Third World Church*, 1983, both published by Inter Varsity Press.

24. E. R. Norman, *Christianity and the World Order*, Oxford University Press 1979.

25. *Instruction on Certain Aspects of the Theology of Liberation*, Vatican City 1984; *Christian Freedom and Liberation*, Vatican City 1986.

26. E. L. Mascall, *Theology and the Gospel of Christ*, SPCK 1977, pp. 16, 23.

27. Juan Luis Segundo, *The Liberation of Theology*, Maryknoll, Orbis Press 1976, p. 7.

28. Gustavo Gutierrez, *A Theology of Liberation*, Maryknoll, Orbis Press 1973, p. 11: 'it is the secondstep . . . it rises only at sundown.' Gutierrez has recently restated this view in his book *On Job: God-talk and the suffering of the innocent*, Maryknoll, Orbis 1988, p. xiii: 'contemplation and practice together make up a *first* act; theologising is a *second* act'; cf. Segundo, op. cit., p. 78.

29. George Orwell, *Inside the Whale and other essays*, Penguin 1979 edn, p. 35.

30. Duncan Hallas, 'Building the leadership', *International Socialism* 40, October–November 1969, pp. 25–32.

31. See Rodney Hilton, *Bond Men and Free*, Methuen 1977; P. Lindsay and R. Groves, *The Peasants' Revolt*, Hutchinson 1950.

32. Christopher Hill, *The World Turned Upside Down*, Maurice Temple Smith 1972.

33. Peter d'A. Jones, *The Christian Socialist Revival 1877–1914*, Princeton University Press 1968; J. R. Orens, *Politics and the Kingdom: the legacy of the Anglican left*, Jubilee Group 1981.

34. See ref. 21 to Chapter 1.

35. Cornel West, *Prophetic Fragments*, Grand Rapids, Eerdmans 1988; Gayraud Wilmore, *Black Religion and Black Radicalism*, Maryknoll, Orbis Press 1983.

36. For the position of the Christian Reconstructionists see *The Journal of Christian Reconstruction* and the publications of the Chalcedon Foundation. Gary North's *Backward Christian Soldiers: an action manual of Christian Reconstruction*, Tyler, Texas, Institute for Christian Economics is a useful guide. For a critical assessment see Sara Diamond, *Spiritual Warfare: the politics of the Christian Right*, Pluto Press 1989. The Christian Reconstruction-

ists held their first British conference at the Hotel Russell in London in September 1989.

37. The publications of the Jubilee Group can be obtained from St Clement's House, Sirdar Road, London W11.

38. *Anglicans and Racism: the Balsall Heath Consultation*, Board for Social Responsibility 1986.

39. Sir Kenneth Lewis, MP, cited in *The Times*, 2 October 1986. The report was published on 9 October!

40. Willard M. Swartley, 'Politics or peace (*eirene*) in Luke's gospel' in Richard J. Cassidy and Philip J. Scharper eds, *Political Issues in Luke – Acts*, Maryknoll, Orbis Press 1983, pp. 18–37.

41. Jim Wallis, *Agenda for Biblical People*, Harper and Row 1976, pp. 1–12.

42. Cited in Richard Gutteridge, *Open Thy Mouth for the Dumb! The German Evangelical Church and the Jews 1879–1950*, Blackwell 1976, p. 283.

43. Andrew Kirk in John Stott ed., *The Year 2000*, Marshalls 1983, p. 16.

44. Wallis, op. cit., pp. 2–3; cf. also his *The Call to Conversion*, Lion 1982, p. 70.

45. See Kenneth Leech, *True God*, Sheldon Press 1985, pp. 304–9.

46. Cited in Ed de la Torre, *Touching Ground, Taking Root*, Catholic Institute for International Relations 1986, p. 93.

47. The literature on the 'underclass' theme is now enormous, particularly in the USA. See W. J. Wilson, *The Truly Disadvantaged*, University of Chicago Press 1987 for a summary of the American material. Frank Field's study *Losing Out: the emergence of Britain's underclass*, Blackwell 1989, is notable for its lack of specific attention to the black community. A forthcoming study by Kaushika Amin and Kenneth Leech for the Runnymede Trust will examine the use of underclass concepts in Britain and the USA.

48. Jon Sobrino, *Spirituality of Liberation*, Maryknoll, Orbis Press 1988, p. 109.

49. MacIntyre, *After Virtue*, op. cit., p. 245.

Index